A VERY MERRY HAPPY
KOSHER CHRISTMAS

A VERY MERRY HAPPY KOSHER CHRISTMAS

A Play

By

Mark Troy

TINSEL ROAD BOOKS

SANTA MONICA, CALIFORNIA

A VERY MERRY HAPPY KOSHER CHRISTMAS

ISBN: 978-0-981943-14-5

Library of Congress Cataloging-in-Publication-Data is available on file.
Library of Congress Control Number: 2009942078

Published by Tinsel Road Books
171 Pier Avenue, #328
Santa Monica, California 90405 USA
www.tinselroad.com

americanforests.org

GL☺BAL
RE☺LEAF

Tinsel Road Books, in association with Global ReLeaf, will plant two trees for each tree used in the manufacturing of this book. Global ReLeaf is an international campaign by American Forests, the nation's oldest nonprofit conservation organization and a world leader in planting trees for environmental restoration.

Produced by Ronnie Marmo and the 68 Cent Crew Theater Company,
A Very Merry Happy Kosher Christmas originally opened at Theatre 68,
Los Angeles, California on the evening of December 4, 2009.

For My Parents.
(who never asked me what I wanted to be when I grow up)

A VERY MERRY HAPPY KOSHER CHRISTMAS was originally produced in Los Angeles, California at Theatre 68 by Ronnie Marmo and the 68 Cent Crew Theatre Company and opened on December 4, 2009. It was directed by Ronnie Marmo; set design by Danny Cistone; assistant set design by Joe Dalo; costumes by Mo Stone; assistant costumes by Melissa Stone; light design by Danny Cistone. Theatre 68 production consultant Crystal Craft. The production stage manager was Caity Engler. The assistant director was Katy Jacoby. The author's assistant was Joanclair Richter. The cast was as follows:

TONY ABRUZZO	Jeremy Luke
CARLO BUMBACHI	Joey Russo
MRS. WEINER	Perry Smith
HAVA ISHMAEL	Shelly Hacco
DOUGLAS	Paul McGee
GARYZINGER	Adam Silverstein
MUHAMMAD	Abhi Trivedi
RABBI NATHAN ISHMAEL	James Engel
DIVINITY LOCKJAW	Monica Quintanilla
LEROY LEE ROY	Greg L. Glass
SHPILKA ISHMAEL	Jeff Blumberg
ZINOBIA ZINGER	Liz Bassford
PATRICIA VANDERBUILT	Regina Palian
BERNADETTE CALABRESE	Katy Jacoby
OFFICER O	Kourtney Sonntag
DETECTIVE ISHMAEL	Peter Newman
ABRUZZO DECONSINO	Clint Tauscher
SHIRLEY MARKOWITZ	Clint Tauscher
HERSCHEL ISHMAEL	Adam Silverstein

CHARACTERS

Tony Abruzzo
Local thug. Stupidest man you could ever meet, but has a heart of gold.

Carlo Bumbachi
Tony's loyal dim-witted best friend. Speaks before thinking.

Mrs. Weiner
Prim, proper tight-lipped librarian with a bit of naughtiness.

Hava Ishmael
Confused young girl looking for love in all the wrong places.

Douglas
A young, studious man with great vision. An innocent, wide-eyed brain.

Gary Zinger
Blind and mysterious. A wildly imaginative Frenchman.

Muhammad
Muslim taxi-driver. Afraid of his own shadow. Deeply in love with Hava.

Rabbi Nathan Ishmael
Hava's father. Pious, virtuous and only wants the best for Hava.

Divinity Lockjaw
Without shame, one of the most talented prostitutes in Manhattan.

Leroy Lee Roy
Divinity's pimp. And he's keeping a big secret.

Shpilka Ishmael
Nathan's rattled and insecure brother.

Zinobia Zinger
The nine-month pregnant wife of Gary who travels by roller skates.

Patricia Vanderbuilt
A washed-up Radio City Music Hall Rockette.

Bernadette Costas
Tony's girlfriend. A free spirited exhibitionist with no direction.

Officer O
Tony's timid first love. First day on the police force.

Detective Ishmael
Nathan's estranged son, Hava's brother. Flamboyantly gay and proud of it.

Abruzzo Deconsino
A Dean Martin-type. Adopted Tony as a baby.

Shirley Markowitz
Leroy's secret on the side. With a not-so hidden secret.

Herschel Ishmael
Nathan and Shpilka's brother.

SETTING

The New York Public Library.
(inside and out)
The time is 1978.
The day before Christmas eve.

"A Very Merry Happy Kosher Christmas" is performed with one intermission.

A Very Merry Happy Kosher Christmas

ACT I

Music blares from all corners of the theater. The Village People's "YMCA."

ON A SCRIM we see written:

New York City, 1978. Winter.

Jimmy Carter is president of the United States. He's a peanut farmer.

The Bee Gees sell 115 million records. All while singing in annoying ear-piercing falsetto.

Studio 54 is the hottest nightclub in the world. And nobody can get in.

"Superman" is the number one movie. The one with Christopher Reeve.

Edward Koch is elected mayor. They call him "hizzoner." He doesn't eat peanuts.

Perrier introduced Bottled Water. Nobody believes it will ever catch on.

CURTAIN: The New York Public Library. Main reference room, second floor.

Shelves and shelves of books going far back to upstage wall as if to infinity. A card catalogue at right, and various halls that lead to more stacks. At left, a window, ice on the pane and crown molding in the ceiling where Christmas lights hang.

Dead center is the librarian's desk. Books, a jar of pencils, along with a black rotary telephone. At the edge, a decorative Christmas tree about four inches high with tiny blinking lights. The librarian MRS. WEINER (pronounced Wi-ner), hair severely pulled back, grey turtle-neck with long brownish dull sweater and black conservative skirt past the ankles reads with HER glasses that dangle from a chain around HER neck.

A Santa in full costume sits on a bench near the stacks – face covered. Also a young girl. 20. Remarkably fresh looking; HAVA ISHMAEL, wearing a Smiley Button and nervously biting HER nails.

At a long table on the other side of the room is DOUGLAS, young, clean-shaven, diligently studying and taking notes never lifting HIS head.

There is man at each far end of the stage. At left: TONY ABRUZZO, 20. Handsome Italian wearing a black ski cap and 70s-era parka. HE lowers the book HE pretends to read – Betty Friedan's "The Feminine Mystique." On the other side of the stage, CARLO BUMBACHI, 20s, with bell-bottoms and platform shoes HE trips over.

SOUND: Light rain falling.

WEINER gets up, goes to the window and closes it. As SHE turns:

TONY drops the book and pulls out a gun pointing it wildly at everyone.

TONY. Nobody move. This is a stick up!

CARLO. (Ranting quickly)This is a stick up, up with your hands, this is a robbery, everyone down on the floor, clear the aisles, down down down...this is a hold-up and the first person to move, takes one in the back, got it?

NOBODY moves or pays attention. WEINER puts HER finger to HER lips:

MRS. WEINER. Shhh. This is a library.

SHE goes back to HER desk. TONY and CARLO look at each other, confused.

TONY. (*Crosses calmly to CARLO*) What'd you just do there? I was doing fine.

CARLO. Oh gosh I'm so sorry, Tony.

TONY. You think I needed help?

CARLO. Oh, no, of course not. I would never think anything.

TONY. You think they needed the whole—(*Mimics*) "This is a robbery, everyone down on the floor, clear the aisles, down down down." That's a little over the top, Carlo.

CARLO. It was. It was way over the top, Tony.

TONY. I mean I had this thing planned out, you know? I worked on this for months. Do you know how many times I worked on my opening? (*Tries various ways*) Nobody move. This is a stick up! Nobody move. This is a stick up! This is a stick up! I had it down cold.

CARLO. You were right, Tony, I had no business being so vociferous.

TONY stares at HIM for a beat.

TONY. What's *dat* mean?

CARLO. I don't know.

MRS. WEINER. *Shhhhh*. This is a library.

TONY. Look. All you did was scare everyone.

THEY look around. Everything is calm.

TONY. Let's just regroup.

CARLO. Regroup, Tony. That's it. Let's regroup.

TONY. We start all over.

CARLO. Got it, Tony. We start over. We regroup. (*To everybody*) We're gonna regroup.

TONY takes the exact position as last time. Erratically pointing the gun.

TONY. Nobody move. This is a –

CARLO. –This is a hold up! My name is Carlo and I'll be your guide.

TONY. Jesus, Carlo, what are you doing now?

CARLO. Just like you said, Tony.

TONY. I said regroup! REGROUP!

CARLO. I thought you meant it in an ethereal way.

TONY. What's dat mean?

CARLO. I don't know.

MRS. WEINER. *Shhhhhh.*

TONY grabs CARLO and moves to a corner, conferring. GARY ZINGER enters: a blind MAN. HE has on dark sunglasses. As HE walks, HE taps HIS white cane on the floor.

MRS. WEINER. May I help you with anything, sir?

GARY. Are you familiar with the name John Merven Carrère?

MRS. WEINER. Well of course I am familiar with the name John Merven Carrère? I am Mrs. Weiner. Head Librarian since 1970. Responsibilities include: business counseling, copy services, exhibition loan program, small resource center, research study, telephone reference and tours.

GARY. You don't say.

MRS. WEINER. John Merven Carrère was partnered at Carrère and Hastings; the architectural firm that designed the library back in 1897.

GARY. Fourteen years to build the joint.

MRS. WEINER. You don't think I know that? I am Mrs. Weiner. Head Librarian since 1970. Responsibilities include: business counseling, copy services –

GARY. (*Pause*) So Carrère's best friend was Charles Le Bargy. A Frenchman. Le Bargy introduced him to the Nizan family. Carrère wanted to do something special for the very pregnant Mrs. Nizan who would later give birth to the world renowned journalist – Paul Nizan. Carrère wrote a letter to the Nizan's stating somewhere in the library he hid a gift. But when Paul died during World War II, they never came to retrieve it.

MRS. WEINER. (*Totally into the story*) What is said to be hidden here?

GARY. One hundred thousand dollars.

MRS. WEINER. (*Loudly*) HUU! (*To herself*) Shhhh!

GARY. Today I am going to find it. I need to do more research on the old issues of *L'Humanité*. The newspaper Nizan eventually wrote for. I am convinced the secret lies within your section of the library. Right on this floor.

WEINER hands all the books SHE's collected and hands them to HIM.

At right, HAVA anxiously looks down the aisles, biting HER nails. CARLO nods at TONY like HE knows what to do and CROSSES to HAVA.

CARLO. Excuse me. My friend over here and I are trying to rob the library –

HAVA. I'd love to help. Really. But I was expecting someone very important, but I guess he's not coming. (*SHE notices*) He's here! He's here! He's here!

SHE jumps up and down with CARLO.

CARLO. He is? He is? He is? Who?

SHE pushes CARLO out of the way and runs up to MUHAMMAD A'LL-HAVE-SECONDS who enters, left. HE has a turban, twice the size of HIS head and a pencil thin mustache. HE speaks with a very heavy Middle Eastern accent:

MUHAMMAD. Hava!

HAVA. You made it! I'm so happy you came.

MRS. WEINER. *Shhhh.* This is a library.

THEY both look around. Obviously.

MUHAMMAD. Of course I came. I haven't missed a day in six months.

HAVA. Six of the happiest months of my life.

MUHAMMAD. Allah never had such a humongous happy six months!

HAVA. Oh, baby. These last twenty-four hours have been the hardest. Look. I'm biting my nails down to the bone. I always bite my nails when I fall for a guy.

MUHAMMAD. And I always have a weird strain of luck when I fall for a gal. Today alone: my Gremlin broke down on Bleeker Street...I had to run the rest of the way here.

HAVA. I'm just glad you made it.

MUHAMMAD. Allah couldn't run this far uptown. Have you told your father about us?

HAVA. I can't. I just can't.

MUHAMMAD. Hava – you promised!

HAVA. My father is a Rabbi. A rabbi. Do you know what that means?

MUHAMMAD. Yes. It means he's going to kill me.

HAVA. And he's so square. When he finds out I've accepted your marriage proposal – it wouldn't be the first time he's disowned a child of his.

MUHAMMAD. He doesn't know the glorious six months we've had. *(Sings very well)* "Summer lovin', had me a blast."

HAVA. "Summer lovin' happened so fast..."

MRS. WEINER. *Shhhh!*

MUHAMMAD. *(Whispers to HAVA)* Allah doesn't have your beautiful voice, Hava. But I have to tell your father that you and I are getting married.

HAVA. He'll flip! Your family is not in our social circle. It's not even in the social circle next to our social circle.

MUHAMMAD. You think those are the reasons – really?

HAVA. And you're Muslim!

Suddenly the Santa lowers the newspaper a leaps to his feet. It's RABBI NATHAN ISHMAEL. Jet black, black beard, payis.

RABBI NATHAN. *Goniff!*

HAVA. Daddy?

MRS. WEINER. *Shhhhh!*

RABBI NATHAN. Muslim!

HAVA. Fiancé!

RABBI NATHAN. Bastard goniff going to take my daughter away? Away from her family? This is outrageous! Do you know who I am? I am a rabbi. And you are a *goniff.*

MUHAMMAD. Sir, please...

HAVA. What are you doing here, Poppa?

RABBI NATHAN. I've been following you, Hava.

HAVA. Stalking me? Like Dudley Moore in "10"? Oh, Poppa...

RABBI NATHAN. – Following you. Like a father who loves for his daughter. Or Richard Nixon looking for dirt in a hotel suite.

HAVA. Why are you dressed like Santa, Poppa?

RABBI NATHAN. I'm working. I took a job from my brother Shpilka.

HAVA. Not Shpilka, Poppa. You know his ideas are too *ongepatcheket*.

MUHAMMAD looks at HER. SHE explains:

HAVA. Outlandish.

MUHAMMAD nods.
RABBI NATHAN. This one works. He discovered that it's hard to hire the Santa Claus this close to Christmas eve – can't find Christians to do it! So he hires Jews.

MUHAMMAD. What's so *ongepatcheket* about that?

RABBI NATHAN. (*Throws MUHAMMAD a look*) The money is good and I can make some extra cash for gasoline. Which I might remind you is up to thirty-five cents a gallon! (*Directly at MUHAMMAD*) Thank YOU very much!

MUHAMMAD. What did I –?

RABBI NATHAN. Now if we could only get our older brother Herschel on board, it could be a family business. Family is very important to me. Which is why I have no idea why you would be with HIM. This...man. What is wrong with kids today? You came back from Vietnam all *farmisht*.

HAVA. I never went to—

MUHAMMAD. (*Overlap*)That wasn't our war, Rabbi...

RABBI NATHAN. You're all into the Bee Gee's. With the open collar shirts and the necklaces. I hear about what you kids do. Smoking.

Staying out all night at the discotheques. Streaking! That's right. A fad. There was a man at Shea Stadium...ran across the entire outfield without his clothes on. They asked him why he did it. You know what he said? "It's fun." Can you imagine that? He did it because it was fun. Now how sick is that?!

MUHAMMAD. Hava. It's time.

HAVA. No, Muhammad.

RABBI NATHAN. *Moe-Ha-Moood*???

HAVA. Poppa. I'd like to introduce you to my fiancé, Muhammad A'll-Have-Seconds.

RABBI NATHAN. This is a name? Muhammad A'll-Have-Seconds?

HAVA. This is his name and I love him.

RABBI NATHAN. How did I raise my daughter? Huh? How? To run off with an Arab?

MUHAMMAD. Not Arab, Rabbi Ishmael. I am Sunni. You see there are Sunni's and there are Shiite's...

RABBI NATHAN. If you start right now, I still wouldn't know the difference for another thirty years! (*Beat*) Neither would anybody else.

HAVA. We met at school, Poppa. Queens College.

RABBI NATHAN. We sent you there for the Jews, Hava, why are you doing this to me?

MUHAMMAD. We didn't plan it, Rabbi Ishmael.

RABBI NATHAN. You didn't plan it. You didn't plan it. They didn't plan the Gaza Strip, but it happened. Thank god, my Hava at least is a virgin.

MUHAMMAD. Oh, we had sex.

RABBI NATHAN. (*Bursting out in prayer*) Sh'ma Yis'ra'eil Adonai Eloheinu...

HAVA. Poppa, please.

MUHAMMAD. Listen to her, Rabbi..

HAVA. It's not what you think.

RABBI NATHAN. Are you *shtupping* him?

HAVA. Yes.

RABBI NATHAN. Then it is what I think. (*Prays*) ...Adonai echad...

HAVA. Muhammad gave me my very first real orgasm.

RABBI NATHAN. (*Stops praying*) This I didn't think. Hava. You are coming home with me. And that's that. You will never see this...this...

MUHAMMAD. I know. *Goniff.*

RABBI Nathan. – Again – you're right.

HAVA. Please be rational...

MUHAMMAD. (*Overlap*)I'm a good man, Sir...

HAVA. No. No, Poppa. I am taking a stand. Muhammad is in my life.

RABBI NATHAN. You say no to your own father? Don't ask me to do to you what I did to your brother Issac, Hava.

HAVA. You disowned him, Poppa.

RABBI NATHAN. He is dead to me now. And you know why he is dead to me?

HAVA. The whole temple knows why he is dead to you, Poppa.

RABBI NATHAN. He is dead to me because he should grow up to be my son. A manly son. He should marry and give me grandchildren.

HAVA. Poppa. He's already come out to you. Issac is gay. Like Liberace.

RABBI NATHAN. Liberace is <u>gay</u>? Who told you that – the *goniff*?

HAVA. Issac has to be who he has to be. Like me. And Muhammad.

RABBI NATHAN. I have to go find a pay phone and call my brother. Tell him he needs to replace me today. I'm taking you home, Havala. And then to the Temple. You need to pray.

HE exits towards a sign that reads Pay Phone, while HE continues HIS prayer.

RABBI NATHAN. *Barukh sheim k'vod malkhuto l'olam va'ed...*

HAVA. Poppa?!?

MUHAMMAD. I'll try to talk some sense into him.

SOUND: A coin drops into a pay phone and it dials.

HE kisses HAVA and exits, right.

HAVA.(*Loudly*) Good luck, my love!

MRS. WEINER. *Shhhhh.*

SOUND: A gunshot.

THEY all turn to see CARLO has shot the gun – and a book comes flying off a shelf. WEINER picks it up; it has a big hole in the center of it.

MRS. WEINER. This. Is. Definitely. Going. In. A. Report.

HAVA. Oh my God!

CARLO. Oh now you get it, eh? Now you know who's calling the shots. Who's in charge. Now you're all gonna do things exactly as I say, got it? Or somebody is going to get very hurt.

TONY. (*Crosses calmly to CARLO*) What'd you just do there?

CARLO. Oh gosh, I'm so sorry, Tony.

TONY. You think I needed help?

CARLO. Oh, no, of course not. I would never think anything.

TONY. I wanted to be the one to shoot the gun.

CARLO. I'm sorry Chief, I just got so excited.

TONY. I'll take it from here.

CARLO. It's all yours, Chief. You are completely in charge. Listen up, prisoners, Tony is now taking over. You're on, Chief.

TONY. Thank you.

CARLO. – And he really means business this time. One word outta your mouths, and bang bang bang...

TONY. ALL RIGHT, CARLO!

MRS. WEINER. This has never happened before. In all my years at the library –

TONY. –Stay cool, librarian lady. Stay cool and you all get to be home for Christmas.

CARLO. And Tony means it. He's almost never salubrious.

TONY. What's dat mean?

CARLO. I don't know.

TONY. All right everyone. I'm in charge.

MRS. WEINER. (*Re: CARLO*) I thought <u>he</u> was in charge.

TONY. Shut up!

GARY. *Bonjour*. Pardon my Italian. Could someone please point me in the direction of the stacks numbered 3224 dash 455 dash 3332 dash 23355 dash 444 dash 5555 dash 4467 dash 8657 dash 4?

CARLO. Oh, sure.

CARLO helps HIM down an aisle of stacks and returns to an angered TONY.

TONY. What'd you just do there?

CARLO. I thought he needed help. He's got a cane.

TONY. Stop helping!

CARLO. You got it, Chief. No more helping. Everybody hear that – no more helping. Go on, Tony.

TONY. Thank you. Now listen up –

TONY notices CARLO's shoes.

TONY. What the hell are you wearing? I said don't look noticeable.

CARLO. This is the hottest thing, Tony. Men's platform shoes. Makes the world look up to me.

TONY. Yeah. Because you look like Cher.

CARLO. Oh. I like her.

TONY. *Fuhgeddaboutit.* Take 'em off.

CARLO takes them off, leaving HIM much much much shorter.

TONY. Now. Everybody listen to me, this is what's gonna happen –

MUHAMMAD and NATHAN enter.

RABBI NATHAN. Hava comes from a Jewish mother. That makes her Jewish. And when her mother lied dying, I made a pledge to her that Hava would marry a Jewish man and give her lots of Jewish grandchildren.

MUHAMMAD. That's what's so beautiful. I've already started trying.

RABBI NATHAN. You're a *gon*—

THEY both stop in THEIR tracks and look at the two men with guns.

MUHAMMAD. Did we miss something special?

TONY. All right, keep moving. Inside. Sit down.

RABBI NATHAN. It's a *meshugana* hold up.

MRS. WEINER. They're robbing a library.

HAVA. Aren't you going to save me, Muhammad?

MUHAMMAD. I don't know. They got pretty big guns.

GARY. (*Pokes HIS head through the stacks*) It's a *Coup d'état*. Pardon my Greek.

MRS. WEINER. Just tell us what you want from us.

TONY. I'm here to learn more about the library.

MRS. WEINER. That's wonderful. I am Mrs. Weiner. Head Librarian since 1970. Responsibilities include: business counseling, copy services, exhibition loan program, small resource center, research study, telephone reference and tours.

TONY. I was using sarcasm. Now everyone stay calm. Carlo.

CARLO. Yeah, Chief?

TONY. We gotta make sure the rest of the hallways are clear. Nobody gets in, nobody goes out. Then we start the plan.

CARLO. You got it, Tony. What is the plan?

TONY. You'll see the plan when it's time for you to see the plan. Now don't do anything until I get back.

CARLO. Promise, Chief.

TONY exits, CARLO whips HIS gun around.

CARLO. All right...now I'm gonna tell you who is boss man in town, got it? *(Puts the gun near MUHAMMAD)* Who's boss man?

MUHAMMAD. You boss man.

CARLO. Yeah?

TONY enters hearing this:

TONY. Did you just? Dammit, Carlo. I wanted to be the boss man.

CARLO. Regroup?

TONY. Regroup!

CARLO. *(To everybody)* We're gonna regroup.

MRS. WEINER gets up from HER desk.

TONY. Where are you going, teach?

MRS. WEINER. It's my lunch break, dear.

TONY. Sit down.

MRS. WEINER. Oh I couldn't possibly do that. It's very important I take my break at the preordained scheduled time per our policy here at the New York Public—

TONY. Sit. Down.

HE waves the gun and SHE sits.

MRS. WEINER. Definitely heading for a formal report about this.

TONY. I'm going to check the other halls. Carlo. I can count on you, right? You make sure nobody does anything. Then we start the plan.

CARLO. You got it, Tony. What is the plan?

TONY. (*Writes note*) You'll see the plan. Now don't do anything until I get back. Can you handle that, Carlo?

CARLO. Promise, Chief.

TONY exits. CARLO walks to HAVA and stomps on HER foot.

CARLO. I'm the mastermind around here.

SOUND: An elevator creaks open.

TONY (*OFF-STAGE*). Oh shoot! (*Enters*) Hurt. Hurt. Hurt.

HE looks at the frozen CARLO.

TONY. What's going on?

MRS. WEINER. He called himself the mastermind.

HAVA. That's right...

MUHAMMAD. He don't listen to you.

TONY. I wanted to be called the mastermind! And now I'm hurt.

CARLO. What happened, Tony?

TONY. Cut my finger. I was taping a note on the elevator door for people not to come in here, and I got me a paper cut.

CARLO. Is there a surgeon in the house?

HAVA. I'm a nurse.

TONY. So you can perform CPR?

HAVA. I could. But you're conscious.

CARLO. It's sometimes hard to tell with Tony...look closer.

HAVA. (*Looks at HIS finger*) You'll be fine.

RABBI NATHAN. Excuse me, Mr. Thief, but I was wondering if I could get home for my evening services?

MUHAMMAD. I never heard of anybody robbing a library. What do you expect to get here?

TONY. Yes, well nobody is as dense as me, eh? Nobody thinks the way Tony Abruzzo thinks. Well it's time to execute my plan.

CARLO. Everybody, keep it down. Here it comes. Tony's plan.

TONY. Where's the safe?

MRS. WEINER. What?

RABBI NATHAN. The what?

TONY. (*To WEINER*) The money, you old broad. Where's you keep the money?

MRS. WEINER. My husband Kenneth and I keep the money in a CD. We get a very good return at the Dime Savings Bank of Williamsburg.

TONY. The safe in here! The money here!

CARLO. You heard him. That's Tony's plan.

MRS. WEINER. You mean the late book fees?

TONY. Yes! Yes! ALL the late book fees.

MRS. WEINER. But we get ten cents a day for late books. And tomorrow is Christmas Eve. There couldn't possibly be more than twelve dollars in the drawer.

TONY. No, no, no, no. This was the perfect plan. A seamless crime. Nobody saw it coming.

MUHAMMAD. Maybe because it shouldn't'a come.

CARLO. There must be some mistake, eh, Chief?

TONY. No guards, no cameras. Count the money, library lady!

CARLO. You heard him. Count the money.

MRS. WEINER. Very well, boss man.

TONY. HEY – I'm the – never mind – just count it!

WEINER counts cash from metal box.

MRS. WEINER. Fourteen dollars and twenty-eight cents.

CARLO. Thank god. More than twelve dollars, it's all okay, Tony.

TONY. Shut up, Carlo. This is a disaster. I'm never gonna get enough money now for the Christmas present I picked out for Bernadette.

NOTE: He pronounces it as Boyn-a-det.

RABBI NATHAN. Is that what this is about? A Christmas present?

MRS. WEINER. Who's Bernadette?

TONY. *Boyn-a-det.* You don't know Bernadette?

MRS. WEINER. Does she have a library card?

TONY. Oh, she's very smart.

CARLO. She's brilliant.

TONY. She's <u>my</u> girl.

CARLO. Bernadette is Tony's girl.

MUHAMMAD. So what's so expensive you need to rob a library to buy her a Christmas present?

TONY. Something she has always dreamed of.

CARLO. (*Raises hand*) I know. I know.

TONY. How would you know?

CARLO. (*Guilty*) I wouldn't know.

TONY. She's always said she wanted a beautiful darling China doll.

HAVA. That's sweet.

RABBI NATHAN. It's a lovely thing.

TONY. And so I'm robbing the New York Public Library so that I can get her one.

RABBI NATHAN. If you don't mind me asking you, Mister *Pisher*, how much do you really need for a little China doll?

TONY. Fourteen thousand dollars.

MUHAMMAD. *Whoa.* That's one big doll.

TONY. Well it's not a doll doll, idiot. What do you think, I'm a moron? I am going to buy Bernadette a Chinese baby.

CARLO. A baby? Like a real baby like in – (*Makes baby sounds*). – Baby?

TONY. Obviously. Ain't it romantic? Bernadette has said it to me a thousand times "I want a China doll, I want a China doll." Clearly she's got the ticking clock. Well we ain't ready to have a baby the old fashioned way – boozing on Ruinite-On-Ice and smoking a *doobie*, so I am going to adopt a baby for her.

CARLO. Tony? Are you sure –?

TONY. It ain't cheap adopting a baby from China. I could get her one from Puerto Rico for like pennies...you can spit in New York and hit a Puerto Rican baby...but Chinese! There's lot of paperwork and plane fares, and lawyers...

CARLO. Tony. I really think Bernadette only meant a little doll – not a real person.

TONY. Well that ain't romantic, dummy! Clearly you know nothing about seducing my Bernadette.

CARLO. Of course not. Your Bernadette is your girl.

TONY. I think I know what my Bernadette wants. And a China doll is just another way of her saying she wants to marry me!

CARLO. Like a euphemism.

TONY. What's *dat* mean?

CARLO. Maybe you're right, Tony, she does want a real baby.

CARLO walks away knowing it's a lie.

TONY. I am going to find fourteen thousand dollars and I am going to order us a China doll! And it's gonna look just like me.

RABBI NATHAN. Only Chinese.

TONY. Exactly. THIS IS MY PLAN. Now...there ain't enough money in late book fees so I'm keeping all of you here for ransom.

HAVA. Ransom? Poppa?

MUHAMMAD. What am I worth?

RABBI NATHAN. Not much.

HAVA. I have to be at the hospital for my shift in two hours.

MRS. WEINER. What about my lunch? There is a strict schedule we follow –

TONY. Nobody goes anywhere. Carlo. Go around and take everyone's wallet.

CARLO. Isn't that against the law, Tony?

TONY. Huh? What? GO!

CARLO does so. Putting all the cash into a paper bag. GARY drops in a coin.

GARY. This is *Coup de grâce*. Pardon my Viennese.

CARLO. This all the cash you got?

GARY. (*Takes off glasses and winks*) I'm expecting more.

MUHAMMAD. Sir? Sir? I cannot be a hostage. I'm not even a citizen.

RABBI NATHAN. He's illegal?

HAVA. Poppa. It's true. Muhammad and I didn't meet at school. He came into the hospital choking on popcorn after a screening of "Jaws 2."

MUHAMMAD. The shark looked real.

RABBI NATHAN. "Jaws 2" scared him? What did he do – pee in his pants during "Smokey and The Bandit"?

MUHAMMAD. I'm sensitive.

HAVA. And a bit of a wimp. I thought at least you coulda rescued me from all this.

MUHAMMAD. He's got a BIG GUN!

CARLO. Tony. You know when Bernadette was over at my place last week she was talking about wanting something for Christmas...you know...without a face. I think she was talkin' about maybe, I don't know...an engagement ring or somethin'.

TONY. What? What young girl would rather have a silly ring then a real honest-to-goodness bed wetting Chinese baby? Are you nuts?

CARLO. Guess I'm wrong. Sorry, Chief.

TONY. Carlo. What was Bernadette doin' over at your place last week anyways?

CARLO. Oh. She was – I don't remember exactly –

Mrs. WEINER. – Well the late book fees divided by two comes to seven dollars and fourteen cents for each of you. Plus the money viciously stolen from all of us... fifteen dollars each on that – comes to a grand total of twenty-two dollars and fourteen cents per criminal. Not quite the crime of the century.

CARLO. Maybe you can pay for the Chinese baby on lay-a-way. You know. First an arm, then a leg. Or maybe they might offer discounts on retarded Chinese babies.

TONY. You're disgusting, Carlo. I am not buying Bernadette a discounted Chinese baby. It ain't right. Gotta think...gotta think... What do I do? What do I do?

RABBI NATHAN. Hey big shot, why don't you rob a library in New Jersey next?

TONY. You people gotta be worth some money. We need to find someone like a Patty Hearst. That's it! (*Stands on a chair*) Is anybody here a member of the Hearst family? (*No response*) Okay. That was worth a try.

CARLO. You know. You shouldn't be greedy. You should really subtract the twenty-two dollars and fourteen cents from the fourteen thousand we've already got, to make it fair.

TONY. Wha'? Where? We? I have to regroup.

RABBI NATHAN. They're gonna regroup.

GARY. Excuse me. But while you are using your time for such a noble cause, I wonder if someone could possibly point me in the direction of the stacks numbered 3456 dash 5656 dash 3111?

WEINER rolls HER eyes and helps GARY to the stacks, upstage.

TONY. I got it! Carlo. Go downstairs.

CARLO. You got it, Chief.

CARLO exits and then comes back in.

CARLO. Why?

TONY. Unlock the gate at the elevator, go down onto Fifth Avenue. Grab the first two people who want to come in and send them up here. And, Carlo. Make sure they're worth fourteen thousand dollars.

CARLO. Is this the new plan?

TONY motions, CARLO gives HIM the Pinky Tuscadero slap and snap, then exits.

RABBI NATHAN. Mr. If-you-don't-mind-you-should-drop-dead, as I mentioned before, it's going to be time for the *ma-ariv* service at the Temple soon...sundown, and I haven't missed an evening service since I'm thirteen. My God formally asks me to pray three times a day.

MUHAMMAD. Six for me.

RABBI Nathan. Oh, you think your God is better than my God?

MUHAMMAD. I most certainly do think my God is better than your God.

RABBI Nathan. You ever hear of the '69 Mets?

MUHAMMAD. Sports?!? You're throwing baseball in my face...what about the Turks!

RABBI NATHAN. How many World Series have they won, *Moe-Ha-Moood!*

MUHAMMAD. MU! MU! MU-HOMMAD! Like the great religion of Islam itself. Promulgated by the Prophet Muhammad in Arabia in the 7th century AD. Yes. Islam meaning "surrender" illuminates the fundamental religious idea of Allah – viewed as the sole God—creator, sustenant, and restorer of the world. *Moe-Ha-Moood!?* It is the will of Allah, to which man must submit, made known through the sacred scriptures of the Qur'an which Allah revealed to his messenger – Muhammad. Muhammad.

RABBI NATHAN. *Moe-Ha-Moood!*

HAVA. Both of you! Stop it! You're making me *ich fil nicht gut*.

SHE crosses and takes the seat across from DOUGLAS and watches HIM work. WEINER goes to TONY waiting for CARLO.

MRS. WEINER. So. You can tell me. I am not just a library technician, I am also a woman.

TONY. (*Looks HER up and down*) Where?

MRS. WEINER. And I happen to know a lot about women.

TONY. How?

MRS. WEINER. Tell me about Bernadette. Why go to all this trouble for her?

TONY. Bernadette is Mother Theresa. With the...with the brains of Jackie Onassis. She's Natalie Wood. And her legs? The undoubtedly sexy legs of the star of that TV show... Cloris Leachman. Her voice is that of Barry White. With a little Carly Simon thrown in. She comes from good Sicilian stock. And not like any girl I have ever dated before. She's prim and proper. She don't swear or punch me in the face at all like some of my other girlfriends. Her father is a doctor. A *gyn-a-cho-lo-gicust*. Those are the lucky ones, cuz they get to look at women's privates all day long. Family is very important to her. I grew up in orphanages, Mrs. *Weener*.

MRS. WEINER. – Weiner.

TONY. – Whatever. One day when I was nine or ten, a man came in. (*When HE says his name, HIS entire body tenses*) Abruzzo. Abruzzo. DeConsino. He adopted me. He told me how he was going to finally give me a home. I would have done anything for him. He sent me out into the streets of Lower Manhattan with his other son – Dodger. Taught me how to lift the wallets out of the pockets of businessmen near Wall Street. And how to sing while I did it!

MRS. WEINER. Isn't that... "Oliver?"

TONY. Hmm?

MRS. WEINER. That's "Oliver Twist."

TONY. No, no. This is different. "I picked a pocket or two."

MRS. WEINER. I think maybe you saw that show when you were young, like it opened in the early 60s.

TONY. (*With realization*) That makes it even worse! Not only did Abruzzo DeConsino ruin my life by keeping me from getting adopted by a nice family – but now I learn I never saw a single dime of royalties from that Broadway show!

RABBI NATHAN. (*Loud for HAVA to hear*) At least Bernadette's Italian. You see how that works, Hava?

SHE rolls HER eyes.

HAVA. (*Smiles, to DOUGLAS*) Hi. My name is Hava Ishmael. I noticed you working –

DOUGLAS. – Douglas. It's nice to meet you. But I'm pretty busy.

HAVA. Are you a student or something?

DOUGLAS. Columbia University. Business scholarship. Actually my parents sent me there to meet a Jewish girl.

HAVA beams then sticks HER tongue out at MUHAMMAD who instantly is jealous.

DIVINITY LOCKJAW, 20, a hot hooker in shorts, shirt tied at the waist, sleeves rolled up, and boots, enters left dropping wet raincoat on a chair.

DIVINITY. I will crush you, man, I will break every bone in your pee little squeaky body, you sick perverted shit-head!

Enter LEROY LEE ROY, Black, handsome in a dangerous way. Oversized fur with purple pimp hat and clothes tie-dyed.

LEROY LEE ROY. (*Singing*) "Ah, freak out – Le freak, c'est chic, Freak out." (*Laughing*) Can you dig it? Come on, girl. Chill. Be cool.

DIVINITY. Hey, I just wanted to get someplace dry, *spaz* – leave me alone.

LEROY LEE ROY. *Fo sho.* I am not asking you, Divinity, I am telling you. I is ordering you.

DIVINITY. Oh you ain't orderin' me shit, Leroy, you better not be orderin' me shit, because nobody orders Divinity Lockjaw to do something like that. I don't do something like that. I don't do it for my momma, I don't do it for my father, and I don't do it for my man.

LEROY LEE ROY. That's you problem, Divinity, you keep thinking of me as your man. You are my employee. You are staff. I be management.

THEY turn. Everyone stares at THEM.

LEROY LEE ROY. Hello peoples. Pardon us. We be having a little office meetin' here as our previous boardroom outside the 42nd Street train station, has become unavailable due to an enormous precipitation of snow.

MRS. WEINER. (*Puts finger to HER lips*) Shhhhhhh.

LEROY LEE ROY. Thank you, I would like a little quiet in here myself while I predispose my below-the-line talent.

CARLO comes running in.

CARLO. Did they come in? (*Re: LEROY and DIVINITY*) Oh great you made it.

TONY. Uhm... Carlo.

CARLO. Yeah, Tony?

TONY. I sent you down to find some people worth fourteen thousand dollars.

CARLO. Minus twenty-two dollars and fourteen cents. And I did. A lovely young entrepreneurial woman and the president and C.E.O. of her company. Did you see the fur on him? You know how many cats had to die for that jacket?

TONY. House cats. That there is a hooker and her pimp, Carlo.

CARLO. Oh jeez, Tony, that ain't worth fourteen thousand dollars minus twenty-two dollars and fourteen cents. I guess I was a little distracted, Chief. You know. On account of the cops outside surrounding the building.

THEY both pause for a second then run to the window.

LEROY LEE ROY. I have asked you to do this one thing, Divinity, one thing, and it's a *cool-o-roonie* idea. Now I get lip?! I get lip?!?

DIVINITY. I should give you more than lip, Leroy, I should give you a nice swift kick in the gonads.

LEROY LEE ROY. Leroy does not believe in physical physicalness against women or men. I am a lover, Divinity. Why can't you be a lover too, and do this one thing for us?

DIVINITY. Because it's vile and disgusting.

LEROY LEE ROY. To you. To you it might be vile and disgusting. But to my big business associates it's a practical way of showing respect. And I charge an enormous amount of money for that respect.

DIVINITY. I am not going to take private dirty pictures of myself and let people see them.

LEROY LEE ROY. Why not, woman? Most of the men below fifty-third street has already gotten to see a peek of that.

DIVINITY. Yeah but now they're all going to trade these pictures–show it to their friends...and their friends. And soon my naked body is out there in the world for everyone to see!

LEROY LEE ROY. But I can make money.

DIVINITY. You make it sound like every girl does this.

LEROY LEE ROY. I think every girl would want to. Show off a little skin, and then sell it? You can't lose!

DIVINITY. You can't protect the pictures. It's bad business.

LEROY LEE ROY. That's where you is wrong, Divinity Lockjaw. I got the head for business. You got the body for making the money for my head for my business.

DOUGLAS. Excuse me –

LEROY LEE ROY. *Watch* you want, dude?

DOUGLAS. I couldn't help but overhear. Are you saying that if there was a way for the entire world to see provocative pictures of your...

LEROY LEE ROY. – Employee's *coochie*.

DOUGLAS. – Employee's...yeah that...that it would be a very good way to make money?

LEROY LEE ROY. And an easy way. Because getting nekked is the easiest kind of work there is. Besides the merchant marines, which I was unfortunately kicked out of due to my race.

DIVINITY. And the fact that you're lazy and I do all the work.

LEROY LEE ROY. There goes that lip again, foxy momma. I am telling you with pictures, you only gotta do it once and just watch the *mulah* roll in. You gotta dig it.

DOUGLAS. Hmmm... I've never dug it.

HAVA. Is that a good idea, Douglas?

DOUGLAS. It's an interesting idea. The pictures, not the digging.

THEIR eyes meet. MUHAMMAD seethes.

DOUGLAS. I'm I'm...working on some new theories about what the future will look like in the twenty-first century.

LEROY LEE ROY. You wanna know what the future will look like. It will look like Divinity Lockjaw without her clothes on, spread eagle on a rainbow comforter with her legs up in the air and two ta-ta's splayed out with people everywhere paying to see that.

DIVINITY. You're getting jack squat from me, Leroy. I hate you. (*LEROY walks away, sotto*) Maybe that's why I love you.

TONY. All right. Fine. We got our hostages. We got our plan. As long as nothing else goes wrong, they gotta deal with us. Now you're sure this place is secure, right?

CARLO. I defy any person to get in here.

SHPILKA ISHMAEL, 50, enters. HE is wearing a reindeer costume complete with antlers that continually knock into things as they are huge.

SHPILKA. Where is he? Where is that brother of mine?!

CARLO. – Except maybe the horse.

SHPILKA. I'm a reindeer, you *putz*, not a horse.

RABBI NATHAN. (*Rises*). Shpilka?

MRS. WEINER. Oh this will not do. First we're held up. Then a ransom is demanded. And now farm animals in the library.

SHPILKA. I'm a reindeer!

CARLO. I thought it was a horse.

MRS. WEINER. Now that I think about it – I don't know if there are any rules against donkeys in the library. Let me check the Librarian's Professional Manual.

SHPILKA. Nathan. It's me. The-not-so-nearly handsome Jewish man who happens to be your brother and worried sick about you. You call me from the New York Public Library and tell me you quit your job two days before Christmas! I need you at Macy's!

RABBI NATHAN. I was following Hava.

SHPILKA. I was sewing my fingers off making a snowman suit for Herschel. You know all the Christians are home with their families. Jews are the only people willing to work this job. What do you expect me to do? This is my high season you know.

RABBI NATHAN. Shpilka, you have to get out of here – the library is being robbed.

TONY. He's not going anywhere.

SHPILKA. Who are you?

TONY. Who are you?

SHPILKA. Rudolph.

HE takes a red nose and attaches it.

CARLO. *Ahh.* Now I see it. He's a reindeer.

SHPILKA. Nate. I don't have time for a robbery. I'm telling you this is a money-making venture that can't fail. Better than the time I thought Jews would take jobs working the pork factories during Lent.

RABBI NATHAN. We've got bigger problems, Shpilka. Hava thinks she's going to marry this Arab.

SHPILKA. An Arab? Like they have in Astoria?

MRS. WEINER. Those are Greeks.

MUHAMMAD. I am Sunni. You see there are Sunni's and there are Shiite's...

SHPILKA. If you start right now, I still wouldn't know the difference for another thirty years! (*Beat*) Neither would anybody else.

HAVA. Both of you are not being fair.

RABBI NATHAN. This is not about fair, Hava. We're Jewish!

TONY. (*Sotto to CARLO*) We're going to have to show the police we mean business, Carlo. Take the new guy and rough 'em up a little.

CARLO. Oh. I can't do that, Tony. I'm against cruelty to animals.

TONY slowly walks to SHPILKA and unceremoniously pulls off his antlers.

SHPILKA. Ouch.

RABBI NATHAN. Shpilka.

SHPILKA. Those were super-glued on.

DIVINITY. There might be other reasons, Leroy, other reasons a girl would do something for a boy. Maybe if I knew you...

MUHAMMAD. – I love you, Hava.

HAVA. You won't even stand up to my father. Or men with guns. You're the weakest Muslim I know!

MUHAMMAD. Well I have no practice at this!

DIVINITY. Leroy. Maybe, perhaps it's not just about business between us.

LEROY LEE ROY. What are you talkin' about, *babe-a-lishis*? I treat you like the fine piece of sirloin you is. I took you to Studio 54. I took you to Plato's Retreat.

DIVINITY. You made me have sex with three other dudes and four girls.

LEROY LEE ROY. But afterwards did we not have spaghetti at Elaine's?

DIVINITY. What have you done for me that didn't involve getting me dates?

LEROY LEE ROY. I bought you a brand new top-o-the-line 8-track player.

DIVINITY. It weighs seventeen pounds. And sounds like a tin can.

LEROY LEE ROY. It be state-of-the-art, Divinity.

DOUGLAS. Excuse me. I couldn't help but overhear. Are you saying that if there was a way for you to get music in a smaller more compact delivery system, you would like that as a gift?

HAVA. You seem very smart.

HE barely smiles and goes back to work.

DIVINITY. I still hate you. I hate you – I hate you! I think I love you, Leroy, as much as I hate you.

LEROY LEE ROY. Love? What are you talking about? You love me? Like Joannie loves Chachi?

DIVINITY. Yeah, just like them.

LEROY LEE ROY. Oh I don't know, Divinity...those TV loves are very powerful. I've never felt that way about any of my workin' girls.

DIVINITY. Maybe I'm different. Maybe I would let you take those Polaroids of me and sell them if I thought you really cared. If you wanted me more. As a lover. Hot and dirty sex. Not like prim and proper all the time like probably what she has. (*SHE points to WEINER*) No offense.

MRS. WEINER. Offense taken.

TONY raises the gun and orders CARLO:

TONY. Cover the door. Nobody comes in or out. Got it?

CARLO. You can always count on me, Tony.

ZINOBIA ZINGER enters left on roller-skates. SHE wears colored knee-highs, runner shorts and is 9 months pregnant. SHE can't stop and goes completely off stage, right.

CARLO. Does that count?

ZINOBIA returns going the other direction and off-stage, left.

CARLO. Yeah that should count.

TONY. Find out who she is and get her in here.

CARLO exits, left.

TONY. I can't even regroup in this place!

MRS. WEINER. (*Looks in big book*) Yup, here it is. In the Librarian's Professional Manual. So many rules about animals allowed in the building. (*SHE looks at SHPILKA*) You are "fixed" right? (*Slams book closed*) I. Am. Calling. The. Police.

SHE picks up the phone and dials.

SOUND: A rotary phone. SHE dials 9 which takes forever to circle back.

MRS. WEINER. Nine.

Then a one...(this takes longer than reality for comedic sake).

MRS. WEINER. One...

TONY pulls the phone from the wall, walk to the window, open it, and throw the phone out.

SOUND: Phone crashing to the cement.

TONY. The cops are already here, lady.

MRS. WEINER. Well they're just gonna have to invent a faster phone.

DOUGLAS looks at HAVA and THEY both smile. HE takes furious notes.

RABBI NATHAN. Excuse us, Mr. The World Revolves Around Me, but how long do you think we're going to have to stay here?

TONY. Until I get my fourteen thousand dollars.

MUHAMMAD goes to HAVA and taps HER.

MUHAMMAD. He's not willing to talk to me. Your father.

HAVA. It would be nice if you acted a little more...pro-active.

MUHAMMAD. I'm a man of peace, Hava.

HAVA. You're weak. Your whole culture is weak. Every time you have to stand up and be a man, you say, "My Holy Qur'an tells me to accept others and love they neighbor." I'm looking for a strong man. (*Smiles at DOUGLAS*)

MUHAMMAD. (*Raging jealously*) We have a future, Hava! My business is taking off!

HAVA. What business? You drive a taxi.

MUHAMMAD. I do more than just drive a taxi. I am the best taxi driver New York City ever had! Go on. Pick two destinations. Any two destinations.

HAVA. Muhammad. I don't like this game.

MUHAMMAD. Come on. Pick.

HAVA. Okay. Jericho Turnpike in Commack to, ah, the Empire State Building.

MUHAMMAD. You're joking. That's a snap! Northern State Parkway to the Satikos, then 495 through the Midtown Tunnel. Make a right – up to 33rd, then a left to Fifth Avenue. Right there.

HAVA. (*Sarcastic*) Amazing.

SHPILKA. That IS pretty good.

MUHAMMAD. I know.

DOUGLAS. What about rush hour?

MUHAMMAD. *Ooooooh.* Handsome college boy has a challenge. Go on.

DOUGLAS. Rush hour – Tremont Avenue in the Bronx to 174th Street in Queens.

MUHAMMAD. East Tremont to Bruchner Boulevard. North. To the Throgs Neck Expressway. Merge on the Cross Bronx. This part is important: Exit on the Clearview...L.I.E. once again...off at Utopia Parkway, straight to 73rd Avenue, left on 1 - 7 - 4!

The entire room breaks out in applauds. Only HAVA is not impressed.

MUHAMMAD. And Hava. Hava, I am going to train all my cousins, and uncles to drive taxis the same way. Going to bring them all over here to America. I'm going to have a fleet! And one day. One glorious day in this amazing city, every single taxi driver will look like me.

RABBI NATHAN. Well that's just ridiculous.

LEROY LEE ROY. No way you gonna take those gigs from no brothers.

HAVA. I told you, Muhammad, that day we met in the hospital, you had to stand up to my father. Now you tell him that we are getting married and you make him believe it, or this is over.

MUHAMMAD. Hava! Please.

HAVA. Abba is right. "I have a dream. A song to sing... to help me through... Most anything..." Someone should really put their music in a show.

DOUGLAS writes that down.

CARLO. Tony, we got no food. Nothing to drink. I'm scared.

TONY. You got the gun, Carlo.

CARLO. I know. But I've never stabbed anyone with it.

TONY. Watch the door. You let me know what's going on.

CARLO. (*Genuinely frightened*) Okay, Chief.

HAVA. (*Whispers to DOUGLAS*) Do you think those guys will really hurt us?

DOUGLAS is too busy writing.

HAVA. I just don't know if I'm making the right decision. I mean, do I give up my entire family for a life with Muhammad? We come from two different backgrounds. Two lives.

DOUGLAS. Look. I'd love to hear about your lovey dovey problems, but I don't really relate to this stuff.

HAVA. To love? How can you not relate to love?

DOUGLAS. Because the future is more important. This is nothing, what we got now. Technology is the future. We are on the cusp of an entirely new industrial revolution. Computers.

HAVA. Oh. We had one of those in nursing school. I couldn't figure it out...all those punch card things...nobody cared.

DOUGLAS. No, no. I am talking about computers in your home.

HAVA. The thing was as big as this building. Besides – what's wrong with what we have now? I just got one of those new touch tone phones. They make a cute beeping sound.

DOUGLAS. Touch tone? That's 1960s out-dated garbage. I have come up with an idea that will put a telephone into every single pocket of every man, woman, and teenager in the world!

HAVA. Who would want to carry their telephone around with them?

DOUGLAS. Everyone!

HAVA. I don't think so. They would be a very long cord.

DOUGLAS. Not corded! Cordless. Cordless! That's it! First I have to invent cordless phones.

HAVA. I still don't see why any of this is more important than love.

DOUGLAS. Think about this: A car that works half on batteries.

HAVA. Why half?

DOUGLAS. It can't run without any gas at all unless the U.S. gets its ass over to that Middle East and takes down a place like Iraq. And I don't think we're going to elect a president stupid enough to do that.

MUHAMMAD. Who is going to invade Iraq? I don't like that idea.

HAVA. Mind your beeswax, Muhammad!

DOUGLAS. Hava, right? Can I admit something to you? I know nothing about love. I don't even know how to talk to a girl.

HAVA. Of course you do.

DOUGLAS. You have nice tits.

HAVA. Yeah you don't know how to talk to a girl.

DOUGLAS. That's why I can't help you with your boyfriend problems. I don't spend much time outside this library. This exact desk. In this very room. Across from Mrs. Weiner. Doing my research day after day, hoping to make the world a better place.

HAVA. You don't date at all?

DOUGLAS. Nope.

HAVA. No girlfriend?

DOUGLAS. Nope.

HAVA. But one needs love to sustain life. Otherwise you wind up, like... Like... (*Holds up her ring*) Look. My mood ring is brown. I'm unhappy. Like you.

DOUGLAS. But I'm not unhappy... <u>am I?</u>

THEY stare into each others eyes.

TONY. (*Looking out window*) This is all for you, my Bernadette.

RABBI NATHAN. He's in love and I have to miss *shul*.

MRS. WEINER. It must be a sick perverted physical kind of love.

TONY. No, no, you're wrong, Mrs. *Weener*.

MRS. WEINER. Weiner.

TONY. Whatever. More than just physical love. It's her soul. I love that girls' soul. I love everything about her. I love the way she sniffs. Uh-huh. Not just her walk, her talk, her smile, I am talking sniff. My Bernadette sniffs like no other person. And at the end of the day all of this will be worth it.

LEROY LEE ROY. It'll be worth a sniff?

DIVINITY. Stay out of it, Leroy. You don't know anything about what a guy would do for his girl.

HAVA. What if you go to prison?

SHPILKA. What if they storm the building? I saw that in a movie.

LEROY LEE ROY. "Dog Day Afternoon."

RABBI NATHAN. That's right. I saw it last week. I got this new machine: Beta. Plays all these funky tapes. It's like having a movie house right in your bedroom. Except the quality sucks and the sound don't work.

DOUGLAS. (*Snaps HIS fingers*) Beta!

SHPILKA. "Dog Day." They killed those robbers in that one.

LEROY LEE ROY. Damn right. Dead as a doors nails.

MUHAMMAD. What about "Midnight Express?"

LEROY LEE ROY. Holy shit man...that dude went to a Turkish penitentiary for some dope...they gonna hang you for taking hostages.

HAVA. Bet you wouldn't go to Turkey for me, would you, Muhammad?

MUHAMMAD. Is this a serious question?

TONY. It's all worth it to buy my Bernadette the best Christmas present she ever seen.

WEINER charges the window.

MRS. WEINER. HELP HELP HELP!!!

SHPILKA. HELP! HELP! HELP!

HE exits left, running for help, passing CARLO.

MAN ON STREET. (*OFF-STAGE*) SHUT UP!

MRS. WEINER. (*Scolding*) YOU. ARE. NEVER. TAKING. A. BOOK. OUT. FROM. HERE. MISTER!

TONY SLAMS the window shut. HE points and WEINER goes back to HER desk.

SOUND: Books crashing to the floor.

TONY. Now what?

PATRICIA VANDERBUILT enters from the stacks. SHE is in a long rain slicker.

TONY. Where the hell did you come from?

PATRICIA. (*With heavy Southern Accent*) Why – Mobile. Alabama, of course.

CARLO. (*Looks down the aisle from where SHE came*) Is Alabama down that way, Tony?

MUHAMMAD. No, it's the I-85 to the I-95 to the 278 through Jersey. Holland Tunnel, you're there.

TONY. *Fuhgeddaboutit.* Okay, sit over there, Mobile, like the rest of them.

PATRICIA. Is there something going on? Cuz I just came in for a few books. On behalf of this fully formed woman from Mobile, Alabama whose state motto is "We dare maintain our rights" —understands the notion that I will be joining the unemployed shortly. One cannot be a Rockette their entire show business career. First her ass falls, then her breasts fall, and then her public relations firm dumps her. I can never take this costume off. I will die.

SHE whips off HER jacket to reveal the costume she wears at Radio City.

SPOTLIGHT: Full dance number. SHE's great but a little old for the gig. Everyone applauds. SHE bows.

PATRICIA. Thank you, thank you kindly.

SHPILKA thinks HE recognizes HER, but doesn't.

COP'S VOICE (*OFF-STAGE*) This is the New York City Police Department. Come out with your hands up.

GARY wanders in, books in hand.

GARY. Geez, I ain't finished in here yet, I wonder if someone could possibly point me in the direction of the stacks numbered 3 –

ZINOBIA rolls in.

ZINOBIA. Gary?

GARY drops all the books.

GARY. Zinobia? What are you doing here?

ZINOBIA. My water broke.

CARLO. Thank god, I'm so thirsty.

GARY. You're having the baby? My wife...she's having our baby!

PATRICIA. Oh heavens.

CARLO. Hey. Someone's coming. God, this day is really going to enervate me.

TONY. What the HELL is with you and this fancy words, Carlo!?

MRS. WEINER. I bet it's my superiors extremely angry about the tardiness of my lunch break.

CARLO. No. It's not library staff.

TONY. Is it the cops?

CARLO. I don't think so.

TONY. Everybody clear the way. If they are going to rush us, there is going to be some fireworks.

CARLO. It's one person. Coming up the back stairs. It's dark out there – hard to tell.

TONY. Man or woman?

CARLO. Woman.

LEROY LEE ROY. Ask her if she needs a job.

CARLO. Oh no. Oh no... no, no, no – I see who it is.

TONY. Well who the hell is she, Carlo?

CARLO. <u>She's a streaker</u>!

RABBI NATHAN. *Vey iz mir.*

LEROY LEE ROY. That be bitchin'!

CARLO tumbles off HIS chair as BERNADETTE CALABRESE streaks across the backstage wall. Each stack, or book, keeps us from seeing HER totally. It is choreographed perfectly. TONY is in shock. HE turns out:

TONY. <u>BERNADETTE</u>?!

Music: The Captain & Tennille, "Love will Keep us Together."

CURTAIN.

<u>*End of Act I.*</u>

ACT II

Music. Abba's "Take a Chance on Me."

ON THE SCRIM we see written:

The top ten fads of 1978 included polyester shirts and growing pot.

The minimum wage: $2.65. Before taxes.

The cover of Playboy for December of 1978 featured Farrah Fawcett.

A dozen eggs cost 48 cents. Soon nobody will be eating them. Cholesterol.

Oh. 1978. Ashton Kutcher is born. It is a great day for all mankind. Especially womankind.

CURTAIN: BERNADETTE sits in the chair at the librarians' desk. SHE is covered with the long brown sweater that WEINER was wearing earlier. SHE holds open the book that CARLO shot with the big hole in the cover, and looks through.

It's cold. The heat has been turned off. HAVA in particular is freezing and huddled in a corner. LEROY holds DIVINITY to keep HER warm. NATHAN and SHPILKA sit at a table.

DOUGLAS is less interested in HIS work by now and mostly watches an unsuspecting HAVA. MUHAMMAD is next to PATRICIA watching HER check out the stacks. But SHE's really just trying to occupy HERself.

MRS. WEINER. (*Nervously looks out window*) They shut the heat.

BERNADETTE. It must be ten below in here.

CARLO. I'm apoplectic!

TONY. Look, Carlo, you're going to tell me what's up with this vocabulary, I'm losing my mind!

BERNADETTE. Leave him alone.

TONY. You protecting <u>him</u> now? After what <u>you</u> pulled in here!

BERNADETTE turns from HIM.

TONY. They think they can beat me. Make me come out. Not going to happen. I stay right here until I get what I want!

HAVA. I'm so cold. I'm frigid. (*Looks at WEINER*) No offense.

MRS. WEINER. Offense taken. (*Looks up at the clock*) We've been stuck here nine hours and thirty-nine minutes. With no lunch.

TONY. Thanks for the update. (*Beat*) Sarcasm.

MRS. WEINER. (*Overlap*) Sarcasm.

LEROY LEE ROY. I tell you's what – I myself could use a nice "Hungry Man Dinner."

SHPILKA. Oh I forgot. I brought snacks.

RABBI NATHAN. Good thinking, Shpilka.

MRS. WEINER. (*Takes HER book*) Now I am sure there is something in the Librarian's Professional Manual that states a no eating policy – (*THEY all stare at HER*) I suppose I can make an exception. I'm famished.

SHPILKA offers EVERYONE the cannolis starting with WEINER.

SHPILKA. I never leave Little Italy without cannolis.

RABBI NATHAN. What were you doing down there?

SHPILKA. I was with Herschel. Trying to get him to join the family business. Tomorrow's Christmas Eve. Do you know how much money

I'm losing being locked up in here? (*Louder so TONY can hear*) Do you know how much money I'm losing being locked up in here?

HE hands CARLO a cannoli.

CARLO. You're very kind.

Then HAVA.

HAVA. Thanks, Uncle Shpilka.

SHPILKA passes MUHAMMAD without offering HIM a cannoli.

DOUGLAS. (*Takes a cannoli and eats*) These are delicious. I'll-have-seconds.

MUHAMMAD. What?

RABBI NATHAN. Mr. I-don't-care-if-you-freeze-your-*tuckas*-off-over-there, how long do you think you can keep us under these harsh conditions?

TONY. That's my business.

RABBI NATHAN. It's going to be sundown soon. I'm going to need to pray.

MUHAMMAD. Me too.

RABBI NATHAN. Him too. Him too. Who'll be listening?

MUHAMMAD. Excuse me? Your God is busy planning a double-header for the Mets!

RABBI NATHAN. My God says "We acknowledge to You, O Lord, that You are our God, as You were the God of our ancestors, forever and ever."

MUHAMMAD. Mine says... "But those who reject Faith and belie Our Signs, they shall be companions of the Fire; they shall abide therein."

RABBI NATHAN. Take this: "Thou art good, for Thy mercies are endless."

MUHAMMAD. Oh yeah? We got "Think not of those who are slain in Allah's way as dead. Nay, they live, finding their sustenance in the presence of their Lord."

RABBI NATHAN. You stole some of that from us!

HAVA. Enough!

TONY crosses to BERNADETTE.

TONY. I do not approve.

BERNADETTE. (*Takes in a huge puff of air; nostrils flaring*) What?

MRS. WEINER. Oh you're "right on" with her. That woman can sniff.

TONY. Just what do you think you were doing, Bernadette?

BERNADETTE. Streaking. The human form is about the most wonderful thing in the world you can share with anyone.

TONY. Wit' ME. Share it wit' me!

HAVA. (*To DOUGLAS*) If I'm going to spend forever with a man, I want to know he shares the same ideas and thoughts and future as I do. And if I decide to streak, he would still accept me.

DOUGLAS smiles then looks at MUHAMMAD who with HIS eyes, drives DOUGLAS lower into HIS chair.

BERNADETTE. (*To TONY*) I am allowed to express myself.

TONY. To who?

CARLO walks past nonchalantly.

CARLO. Yo, nice ass, Bernadette.

BERNADETTE. Thank you, Carlo.

TONY. You saw? Not the ass. Not the ass.

BERNADETTE. It's mine. And I can do whatever I want with it.

TONY. Hey. Hey! I demand to know why you did it, Bernadette, I demand to know what you were doing here, *witout'* your undergarments!

BERNADETTE. It's – fun.

RABBI NATHAN. You see how sick that sounds.

HAVA. Poppa!

TONY. What are the odds anyway that I happen to be at the main branch public library on the same day you come streaking through?

BERNADETTE. I don't know. I streak through here everyday.

TONY. What?

BERNADETTE. I'm a woman, Tony. And I am spreading my wings.

CARLO walks past nonchalantly.

CARLO. More than just your wings, Bernadette.

TONY. CARLO! (*To BERNADETTE*) I forbid you to do this ever again! Running naked in public is crazy.

BERNADETTE. Oh? And taking hostages in a library is SANE?

TONY. We gonna be husband and wife one day, Bernadette, I can't have you runnin' around New York City doin' this kinda thing. You're gonna have to follow my rules.

BERNADETTE. I have to follow your rules?

TONY. Dat's what women do for men. They follow rules. When I slip that ring on your finger, there is going to be a commitment between us. And with that comes a collection of conditions.

BERNADETTE. Is that so? Well I haven't even seen any ring, Tony. Have I? Have I, Carlo?

CARLO. I'd like to stay out of it.

TONY. Stay out of this, Carlo.

CARLO. That's what I'm doing, staying out of it.

BERNADETTE. I have not seen a ring and therefore I am free to do as I please.

TONY. Bernadette. Don't be angry. I am planning the most wonderful, fabulous Christmas you have ever had.

BERNADETTE. Does it start with me being held hostage in a library?

TONY. Yes. It seems to have. But I can't let you go just yet. It'll look like I was playin' favorites with ya. You know? So we'll hang out here until it all gets figured out. And then we can talk about more important things... Movin' in together. Marriage. <u>Family</u>?

BERNADETTE. Oh you're talking kids already?

CARLO giggles.

BERNADETTE. What's so funny, Carlo?

CARLO. I'd like to stay out of it.

TONY. Stay out of this, Carlo.

CARLO. That's what I'm doing, staying out of it.

TONY. You know how I feel about family, Bernadette. I don't have a family, remember? Never did. You would be my family. And our family will be our family.

BERNADETTE. Abruzzo was your family, Tony.

TONY. (*HIS entire body tenses*) Abruzzo. Abruzzo.

BERNADETTE. Not this again. Everyday the same thing.

TONY. He was the person who told me that my mother abandoned me because I was an ugly baby and she thought she could do better, so she ran off with a Toyota dealer and had apparently very pretty girls.
BERNADETTE. You've got to get over it, Tony. The whole thing was a misunderstanding...he tried to do good by you.

TONY. I was his pawn. No, no. You are my family, and in my family the woman does not work.

BERNADETTE. I want to work.

TONY. Or streak.

BERNADETTE. I want to streak.

TONY. You stay home –

BERNADETTE. – And be barefoot and pregnant?

CARLO. Well you won't have to be pregnant, that's all been figured out.

TONY glares at HIM.

CARLO. I'd like to stay out of it.

TONY picks up a book and pops CARLO on the head with it.

CARLO. AW!

MRS. WEINER. All right – from now on I am assessing a damaged book fee.

BERNADETTE. What kind of life would that be for me, Tony? For us? I have dreams too. And let's face it, your job opportunities are limited.

RABBI NATHAN. After today, they're probably *facoct.*

BERNADETTE. There are very few things you know how to do, Tony.

TONY. That's not true. I can...I...I can...I'm good at hustling people.

BERNADETTE. That's not much of a vocation. You've lost five of the last five jobs you've had.

TONY. They weren't suited to me.

BERNADETTE. Pizza maker?

TONY. Racist. Racist to assume that because my name is Anthony Abruzzo that I should be able to make pizza.

BERNADETTE. Well I think starting with your masterful invention of mashed potatoes and cucumber pizza was not a good beginning.

TONY. It could become popular.

BERNADETTE. You got fired from the construction site.

TONY. Banging gives me a headache.

BERNADETTE. The cement company.

TONY. I got scared I'd find Jimmy Hoffa in the mix. It's been five years.

BERNADETTE. You're not good at anything, Tony.

TONY. I'm good at loving you.

BERNADETTE. (*Smiles lovingly*) I have to watch out for my own future, you know? I knew you would do something like this one day.

TONY. It's not what you think, Bernadette. I did this all for you.

BERNADETTE. Me?

TONY. For your Christmas present.

BERNADETTE. Is this about the engagement ring I wanted? I was just day-dreaming, Tony. You robbed a library for an engagement ring?

TONY. Don't be stupid. I wouldn't have robbed a library for an engagement ring. I robbed the library to buy you a Chinese baby off the black market. You know, the China doll you always wanted.

BERNADETTE. I only meant a little doll, not a real person.

TONY throws CARLO a look.

BERNADETTE. A CHINESE BABY?

CARLO walks past nonchalantly.

CARLO. When he says it out loud, it don't sound so romantic.

TONY practically throws HIMself over a table, to strangle CARLO.

GARY helps ZINOBIA in, still on HER roller-skates.

ZINOBIA. Sorry that was such a long pee, Gary.

GARY. I've never seen a woman pee that long. And standing up!

ZINOBIA. I was on my way to Lennox Hill Hospital when I saw your note on the kitchen table. Not here, Gary. Not here on that ridiculous silly treasure-hunt again. Going through old warn-out issues of that stupid magazine.

GARY. L'Humanité. I've tracked down John Merven Carrère to this section of the library. The money is here.

ZINOBIA. Isn't your family more important? I'm giving birth to a new generation of Zinger's! Gary Zinger. Zinobia Zinger. And I'm thinking...and this took a lot of thought... Zinobia Jr. Zinger.

GARY. That's a terrible name.

ZINOBIA. For a girl?

GARY. For a human.

ZINOBIA. Well I don't see you trying to come up with a name, Gary.

GARY. Any name is fine. Greg. Bobbie, Peter.

ZINOBIA. (*Bawling*) You want to name our baby after one of the "Brady Bunch" boys. I'm the one at home getting the baby's room ready, putting the crib up. You're too busy with your adventures and *cockamamie* money-making schemes.

GARY. Some of my ideas were good. Hiring Jewish Santa's – that coulda worked. Alright then. Fine. You pick a name.

ZINOBIA. I'm thinking...and this took a lot of thought. Zeena Zinger.

GARY. That's a terrible name.

ZINOBIA. Because the kids will tease her at school.

GARY. No. Because I'll tease her at home.

ZINOBIA. (*Breathing heavily*) You know that feeling you get after the meatball parmigiana at Ray's Pizza?

GARY. The gas build up, back pain, and acid reflux?

ZINOBIA. Same feeling when a baby is coming out of your vagina. (*Panics*) Oh my god, oh my god.

HAVA rushes over.

HAVA. It's okay. I'm a nurse.

TONY. Yup, she's very good.

THEY stretch out ZINOBIA on the floor.

ZINOBIA. I'm thinking...and this took a lot of thought... Zola Zinger.

HAVA. That's a terrible name.

GARY. Listen to her. She's a nurse.

Lights up on a street. 5th Avenue.

OFFICER O'REILLYHULAHANO'BRIEN; a petite young female cop in uniform. SHE speaks through a bullhorn but HER voice is thin and crackling.

O'REILLYHULAHANO'BRIEN. This is the New York City Police Department.

TONY and CARLO panic. TONY opens the window.

SOUND: Pigeon flapping near the window.

HE uses a book to "shoo" it away.

TONY. What?

O'REILLYHULAHANO'BRIEN (*Not that much louder. And with no confidence*) This is the New York City Police Department.

CARLO. I think it's the police department.

TONY. They should use a bullhorn.

A Very Merry Happy Kosher Christmas

O'REILLYHULAHANO'BRIEN. (*Barely audible*) I am using a bullhorn.

TONY. (*To CARLO*) They are using a bullhorn.

TONY grabs HAVA and puts the gun to her head.

RABBI NATHAN. What are you doing to her?

MUHAMMAD. Hava!

TONY. (*Out the window*) Don't come any closer, copper!

O'REILLYHULAHANO'BRIEN. I'm not coming any closer. I'm afraid of being shot.

TONY. I could snap at any second!

O'REILLYHULAHANO'BRIEN. Would it be possible to snap after my shift, it's my first day.

TONY. They sent a rookie?

CARLO. Tony. They're not taking us seriously.

O'REILLYHULAHANO'BRIEN. No. We are taking you seriously, it's just that for the last 9 hours, the other cops have been busy surrounding the building and preparing to shoot you in the face, and since I'm inexperienced, they let me hold the bullhorn.

TONY. They wanna shoot off my face?

O'REILLYHULAHANO'BRIEN. They're only going to start with you face, but then probably work their way down.

TONY. I like my face.

CARLO. It's a nice face, Tony.

O'REILLYHULAHANO'BRIEN. I tell ya: most of the precinct laughed their asses off that two bozos robbed the New York Public Library.

TONY. Jesus. They're laughing at me.

BERNADETTE. Because you're an idiot.

TONY lets HAVA go. MUHAMMAD opens HIS arms, but SHE goes to DOUGLAS instead.

O'REILLYHULAHANO'BRIEN refers to HER notes:

O'REILLYHULAHANO'BRIEN. I believe protocol demands I should get your name.

TONY. Tony.

O'REILLYHULAHANO'BRIEN. Not Tony Abruzzo from Sheapshead Bay.

TONY. I <u>am</u> Tony Abruzzo from Sheapshead Bay.

O'REILLYHULAHANO'BRIEN. Cuz there is no way I want to deal with Tony Abruzzo from Sheapshead Bay.

TONY. What's wrong with Tony Abruzzo from Sheapshead Bay?

O'REILLYHULAHANO'BRIEN. That jerk took me to our senior prom, then ducked out before midnight and I never got a kiss.

TONY. Odharnait?

O'REILLYHULAHANO'BRIEN. (*Only slightly louder*) Hi, Tony Abruzzo from Sheapshead Bay. It's Officer Odharnait O'ReillyhulahanO'Brien at yer service.

TONY. You got married. Congrats.

O'REILLYHULAHANO'BRIEN. First to Gillian O'Reilly, then Gus Hulahan, and finally Mickey O'Brien.

TONY. I'm glad it all worked out for ya, Odharnait.

O'REILLYHULAHANO'BRIEN. What work out, Tony? None of the marriages lasted more than three months.

TONY. Hey, I don't think it's so fair to put all your troubles on my head, you know. The honest to god truth is, the only reason I didn't kiss you that night was because you were so damn hideously ugly.

BERNADETTE. Nice going, Tony.

CARLO. Wow. I don't think she's so damn hideously ugly now.

TONY sticks his head out the window.

TONY. How do you like that – she's blossomed into a beautiful woman.

O'REILLYHULAHANO'BRIEN. (*Refers to HER notes*) I believe protocol demands I should find out if you have any weapons up there so I can get a bead on the number of bodies that might pile up. That last part I'm pretty sure shouldn't be said out loud.

TONY. (*To CARLO*). What happened to us? We were never bad kids.

BERNADETTE. You have to turn yourself in, Tony.

TONY. Not until I get my money for your Chinese baby.

BERNADETTE. Oh god.

During the previous, everyone has decided to sneak out, but only get as far as the door when TONY turns:

TONY. Hey! Where the hell are you all going? Get back! Get back inside!

THEY all come back in and are seated. TONY goes to the window:

TONY. Odharnait! I need fourteen thousand dollars to buy a Chinese baby for my girl Bernadette.

O'REILLYHULAHANO'BRIEN. Not Bernadette Calabrese from Borough Park.

TONY. It is Bernadette Calabrese from Borough Park.

O'REILLYHULAHANO'BRIEN. Cuz there is no way I want to deal with Bernadette Calabrese from Borough Park. She streaks through this freakin' library every day and we can never catch her.

BERNADETTE. That's because I'm built for speed.

TONY. (*Holds back tears*) You saw her naked too!? Oh, Odharnait. Isn't there something you could do to get me out of this jam? For old times sake?

O'REILLYHULAHANO'BRIEN. Yeah, well next time pucker up, buddy, and you won't find yourself being made fun of by the entire 12th Precinct. Now unfortunately, you're gonna have to deal with the department's most difficult hostage negotiator.

TONY. Not a hostage negotiator. Not a hostage negotiator!

Lights off on street.

CARLO. Tony. What have we gotten into? What if the police start shooting? Or take us to Sing-Sing. I can't sing!

TONY. Calm, Carlo. I'm going to get that money and prove to Bernadette I'm good at somethin'.

LEROY slowly strides to BERNADETTE.

LEROY LEE ROY. Allow me to introduce myself. Leroy Lee Roy. Charmed, sugar.

BERNADETTE. Bernadette Calabrese.

LEROY LEE ROY. How much money does a girl like you make? I don't mean to pry, but I couldn't help but notice when you came in earlier.

BERNADETTE. Sorry for airing my dirty laundry with my boyfriend.

LEROY LEE ROY. I was referring to your amazing buttocks.

BERNADETTE. I don't have a job right now. Not sure what I want to do.

LEROY LEE ROY. Perhaps you would consider working for *moi*.

BERNADETTE. (*Looks at TONY to piss HIM off*) Perhaps I would.

TONY. Okay, okay... That's enough!

BERNADETTE. Oh excuse me, Tony, now I have to run it by you every time I want to talk to somebody?

TONY. Not the pimp! Not the pimp!

BERNADETTE. Or maybe I should ask my new Chinese baby – except – I DON'T SPEAK CHINESE!

TONY turns and walks past WEINER who shakes HER head at HIM.

TONY. *Shhhhh!* This is a library!

DOUGLAS notices how cold HAVA is. HE walks over to CARLO, rips off HIS ski cap and puts it on HER. CARLO looks up – not even realizing what happened. SHE smiles. DIVINITY walks over to DOUGLAS.

DIVINITY. What's your name?

HAVA. (*Territorially*) It's Douglas.

DIVINITY. Wanna date, Douglas?

DOUGLAS. When would that be? I'm pretty busy with my studies.

DIVINITY. It would be...now. I rarely book ahead.

DOUGLAS. *Hmm.* I would really rather shower and feel better about myself before we date. I would also buy you flowers and candy. Maybe take you to a nice movie...Oh – you know what just opened... "Norma Rae" – we can see that. And then maybe dinner and a...

DIVINITY. Yeah, you're time is already up.

SHE walks away.

HAVA. I'd love to see "Norma Rae."

MUHAMMAD watches HAVA, jealously.

DOUGLAS. Maybe after I work more on my inventions. Inventions are my bag.

DIVINITY. Oral is mine.

HAVA. (*To DIVINITY*) I thought bending over cheap hotel room dressers and buying fruit flavored condoms was your bag?

LEROY LEE ROY. Oh she got you, honey.

MRS. WEINER.(*To DOUGLAS*) So you got lots of ideas, do you?

HAVA. Douglas is very smart.

DOUGLAS. Not really. But yeah.

HAVA. Tell them about the music. Go on. It's good.

DOUGLAS. I think in the future all music will NOT be on 8-track.

LEROY LEE ROY. You mean we'll just memorize it? (*Laughs*)

DOUGLAS. No. I believe music and many other things will be digitized.

DIVINITY. Never heard of it.

LEROY LEE ROY. That's because you work for me. And if I never heard of it, then you's never heard of it.

DOUGLAS. Look at this. (*HE rolls out maps*) Maps. That's one of my ideas. Maps. All in one place.

MRS. WEINER. Like a book of maps? We have those, third floor, aisle seven.

MUHAMMAD. What the hell do you need maps for – you got me!

DOUGLAS. No, no. Better. Electronic maps. In your car. Or... Better yet...in the palm of your hand.

CARLO. I wish I had a map in the palm of my hand. (*Stares at HIS palm*) Where would I go? I'd go to my thumb.

DIVINITY. Why do we need maps so...convenient, Douglas?

DOUGLAS. (*Long pause*) Convenience.

RABBI NATHAN. It's an interesting idea, young man.

DOUGLAS. There are so many new things on the horizon. I can see them. Right here in this very room. In thirty years, this room will be totally different. You see...you see these card catalogues? In the near future, I think I could come up with a way to put them all on computer. Every book in this place...on a computer no larger than that desk. There will be no card catalogues. What would we do then?

MRS. WEINER. I would punch you in the face.

DOUGLAS. No. Don't you see how easy it will be to find research? In fact people will probably just stay home and have computers right there and never ever ever have to even come to a stupid library.

WEINER leaps over the table –

MRS. WEINER. You mother-fuc—

EVERYONE pulls HER back down.

TONY. – Break it up! Break it up!

BERNADETTE. Tony. I think we should talk. I've been keeping something from you.

Lights up on street.

O'REILLYHULAHANO'BRIEN (*Through bullhorn, still soft-spoken*) Tony. It's me again. O'ReillyhulahanO'Brien.

TONY. (*Runs to the window*) Where is Ed Koch with my fourteen thousand dollars?

O'REILLYHULAHANO'BRIEN. The hostage negotiator is here.

CARLO. Tony. Let's give up.

TONY. What are you talking about? We're so close I can taste the Chinese food my little baby's gonna cook for me already.

CARLO. I don't want the money. I don't live for money or expensive gifts or human trafficking like you do. I live for love.

TONY. Love? Carlo, I never even seen you with a steady girl. You're always the third wheel with me and Bernadette.

CARLO. Yeah well, that's the thing, Tony. I kinda sorta love Bernadette.

TONY. What? (*Turns to BERNADETTE*) Did you know this?

BERNADETTE. He's talked to me about it, Tony. But we never did anything.

TONY. You better not a done anything. Carlo and you? It's laughable!

BERNADETTE. I ain't laughing.

CARLO. I think I know Bernadette. I know she wants to be an independent, modern woman. And she doesn't want to be a housewife. I know she likes to streak. I know she likes guys who are smart. And have big vocabularies. You know, an innovated lugubrious way of speaking.

TONY. You learned all those fancy words for <u>my</u> Bernadette?

BERNADETTE. He did it for me and didn't go behind my back to do it, like trying to adopt a black market baby.

TONY. It won't be black, it'll be Chinese.

BERNADETTE. I just wanted an engagement ring, Tony. A cheap one. Just to show me you cared. But you're always going way over the top. Trying too hard to impress me. Like taking over the library. Carlo is simple.

CARLO. I'm a simpleton.

SHPILKA. You can say that again.

CARLO. I'm a simpleton.

RABBI NATHAN. The two of them together are a regular *yin* and *yin*.

CARLO. I just want to be happy. With Bernadette. And make a nice living...

TONY. Making pizzas, Carlo. Making pizza. What kind of job is that for a nice Italian boy from Sheapshead Bay?

CARLO. That's my dream.

TONY. I guess my dream is different, eh? My dream is bigger. To be with Bernadette. To show her a life she deserves. And I'm going to do it. No matter what it takes. (*Screams out to the street*) Bring it on, O'ReillyhulahanO'Brien. Bring on your big fancy *schmancy* hostage negotiator...he ain't got a chance with me. I don't get my money – I start killing the hostages – and this starts getting serious!

Enter street— DETECTIVE ISSAC ISHMAEL. HE grabs the bullhorn and is as gay as they come – but covers it well.

DETECTIVE ISSAC. Give me that. Tony. It's hostage negotiator Detective Issac Ishmael. Let's end this thing. Come on out. "I ain't packin' nothing, see?"

HE opens HIS jacket and has five guns in plain sight.

HAVA. Is that Issac? Poppa!

MUHAMMAD. Your brother Issac?

RABBI NATHAN. *Oye gevalt.*

HAVA. Poppa... Issac is here to save us.

GARY. We've got to get Zinobia to a hospital.

ZINOBIA. I'm thinking...and this took a lot of thought...no wait that sucks too.

RABBI NATHAN. Hava. That boy is dead to me. Your brother is dead to me. (*HE rips the Santa suit*) Dead.

SHPILKA. Nathan! It took three days to sew that suit.

DETECTIVE ISSAC. Tony. I need you to talk to me.

TONY. I ain't coming out. And if I don't get fourteen thousand dollars, I start shootin'. "Now get somebody in charge here."

DETECTIVE ISSAC. Stay cool, Tony. Everyone is going to get out of there just fine, and you're gonna get what you want. (*To O'REILLYHULAHANO'BRIEN*) He ain't gonna get what he wants. Get guys up on the roof. We give 'em twenty minutes, then we storm the joint. Start the clock.

O'REILLYHULAHANO'BRIEN. Cutbacks, sir. I didn't bring a watch.

Lights out on street.

LEROY catches HAVA's eye.

LEROY LEE ROY. Allow me to introduce myself. Leroy Lee Roy—

SHE slaps HIS face and walks away.

LEROY LEE ROY (*CONT'D*) Wha'? Damn girl, I was also throwing in medical insurance!

DIVINITY. Why don't you just leave people alone, Leroy?

SHPILKA watches PATRICIA do some stretching exercises. With HER head upside down, SHE looks up at HIM.

SHPILKA. Hadassah, it IS you. Don't you recognize me?

PATRICIA. I might be a simple girl from Mobile, Alabama...whose state flower is a Camellia, but I could never forget you, Shpilka. And I don't go by Hadassah Morgankvelts anymore. My background in Mobile, Alabama, population 197,055, taught me that in order to reinvent oneself, one must completely overhaul.

SHPILKA. What was wrong with Hadassah Morgankvelts? It's a beautiful name.

PATRICIA. Do you really want to go to Radio City Music Hall and watch Hadassah Morgankvelts in tight leggings kicking her sexy, well worked-out legs up into the air?

SHPILKA. It would give me an erection. Depending on where my seats were.

PATRICIA. I want you to know, Shpilka, that a day hasn't gone by when I haven't thought of you. Or the hills of Mobile, Alabama.

SHPILKA. And to think it took a hostage situation for us to meet again.

PATRICIA. So much time has passed.

SHPILKA. For me it was standing still. Why didn't you call me, Hadassah? Find me? We had a beautiful night together.

PATRICIA. One night. <u>One</u> simple night. Neither one of us was ready to change our life over that one simple night.

SHPILKA. But I never married. Never had a family. After that night I never stopped praying we would be together, that we would reconnect.

PATRICIA. But you did have a family, Shpilka. (*Beat*) We had a son.

SHPILKA. A *boychik*?

RABBI NATHAN. Shpilka?

PATRICIA. A child of the great growing South. Yachleel Zerubbabbel.

SHPILKA. THIS is what you named our son?

PATRICIA. Yachleel Zerubbabbel Ishmael. After your father.

SHPILKA. My father – Dave?

PATRICIA. Maybe I misheard. But it happened. And sure enough nine and a half months after that night, a beautiful bouncy boy – Yachleel came out of my loins striking an incredible likeness to a not-so-nearly handsome Jewish man.

SHPILKA. Nine and a <u>half</u> months?

PATRICIA. It was a particularly difficult pregnancy. You going to hate me for that too, Shpilka?

SHPILKA. I don't hate you. Never. No. Where is he, Hadassah? Where is my son Yachleel Zerubbabbel Ishmael?

PATRICIA. I gave him up for adoption. I don't know where he is now.

SHPILKA. Well with a name like that – I hope not Catholic school.

PATRICIA. I've ruined our lives, Shpilka. By giving him up – by not finding you – I've ruined our lives.

SHPILKA. One night of passion and this is what we get? Yachleel Zerubbabbel Ishmael. We must find our beautiful little boy.

HE turns to NATHAN who has overheard it all and comes to HIM for a hug.

TONY. (*Out the window*) Hey, pig. What's going on out there?

Lights up on street.

DETECTIVE ISSAC. (*Nods. Into bullhorn*) You don't have to call me names, Tony. I'm trying to help. We have somebody here for you to talk to.

TONY. I ain't talking to nobody.

DETECTIVE ISSAC. It's Abruzzo DeConsino.

SOUND: Ominous musical chord.

O'REILLYHULAHANO'BRIEN exits and returns pushing a wheelchair with ABRUZZO DECONSINO aboard. HE is handed the bullhorn:

ABRUZZO. Is that you, Tone?

TONY. (*HIS entire body tenses*) Abruzzo. Abruzzo.

ABRUZZO. Tony. Please. Talk to me.

TONY. The man who ruined my life.

ABRUZZO. No. No – I gave you a life. I gave you my name. My name is your last name...I gave it to you. Tony Abruzzo.

TONY. I picked a pocket for you!

ABRUZZO. Isn't that "Oliver"? Tony, whatever you think I did to you, I can make up to you. Tony.

TONY. No. There is no way you could ever in a million years make it up to me.

ABRUZZO. I found your father.

TONY. You just made it up to me.

ABRUZZO. I bribed a doctor at the hospital you were born in. I have your father's name. After all these years.

TONY. What is it? Is it Tony?

ABRUZZO. No.

TONY. Is it Italian?

ABRUZZO. No. But it's very recognizable. I don't think you'll have any trouble finding him in New York City. It's Shpilka Ishmael.

TONY. It is? Shpilka Ishmael?

DETECTIVE ISSAC. Shpilka Ishmael? That's my uncle. Uncle *Shpilky*?

SHPILKA.(*Crosses to the window*) I'm here! Help! I'M in here! With your father. And Hava. Help us!

DETECTIVE ISSAC. Poppa? Are you in there?

NATHAN turns away.

DETECTIVE ISSAC (*CONT'D*). You're not speaking. You <u>must</u> be in there. Poppa listen to me. (*Suddenly more gay*) I want you to know I'm proud of who I've become. The first openly homosexual New York City Police Detective. I told them it's not their business. Don't ask. Don't tattle – that's my motto. Besides. (*Very gay*) People hardly notice.

O'REILLYHULAHANO'BRIEN. I noticed.

DETECTIVE ISSAC. Shut up. It's okay that I'm dead to you, Poppa. I still have my friends on the force. And my life partner. A fireman at a Brooklyn house with an incredible hose. *Whoo-hoo.* But you can't hurt me anymore. I'm strong. I'm happy. I'm alive. You can throw away your family. Disown me. Disown Hava. But you'll be left alone, you know that. All alone. (*Holding back tears*) Oh, Poppa...I don't want us to fight anymore.

RABBI NATHAN. I don't want you to be gay anymore.

DETECTIVE ISSAC. Can you not accept me for who I am? For the man I am. For what God made me?

RABBI NATHAN. God made you a *fegela*?

DETECTIVE ISSAC. I have accomplishments, Poppa. I have risen the ranks in my job. I am a valued member of my community. I am respected. I am loved. My apartment is tastefully decorated in pastel colors. And I won't change even for you, Poppa.

RABBI NATHAN. We don't have to fight. We just don't have to talk to each other.

DETECTIVE ISSAC. Maybe that's not good enough anymore, Poppa.

RABBI NATHAN. Maybe it's not. Issac.

ABRUZZO. So, Tony. If you could forgive me... I think we could end this.

TONY. I forgive you.

ABRUZZO. Tony. Let the hostages go.

TONY. No. Yes. No. I'm all confused. First Bernadette and Carlo, then fourteen dollars and twenty-eight cents in late book fees, a gay cop...and...are you sure you're Shpilka Ishmael?

SHPILKA. I'm Shpilka. Your Poppa.

TONY. (*Eyes welling up*) Yes. Yes! A family. A history. Jesus Mary Mother of God – finally – I can get *Bat Mitzvah'd*!

RABBI NATHAN. Hey, Mr. Murdering Rampage Hostage Taker: *Mazel Tov*.

SHPILKA. Wait. Wait. There's someone else you need to mee—. (*Looks around, no PATRICIA*) Uhm... This. This is your Uncle Nathan.

TONY. My uncle Nathan is *Santy Claus*?

RABBI NATHAN. And your cousin. My daughter Hava.

TONY. You're beautiful, Hava. Beauty runs in our family. But Father? Father – do you know where my mother is?

SHPILKA shakes HIS head. TONY breaks down as MUHAMMAD crosses to NATHAN.

MUHAMMAD. I noticed you took the Italian into the family.

NATHAN ponders this as LEROY crosses to DIVINITY about to spill his heart when:

SHIRLEY MARKOWITZ (*OFF-STAGE*) Where is my man?! Where is he?

A transvestite, SHIRLEY MARKOWITZ, enters: HE is a man. Dressed like a woman but not even trying that hard. The high-pitched voice goes in and out on occasion and SHE clearly has not spent that much time in heels.

SHIRLEY MARKOWITZ. I know he's in here... I followed him all the way from Times Square! I broke through police barricades. And look – in heels!

LEROY ducks behind NATHAN.

SHIRLEY MARKOWITZ (*CONT'D*). Where is Mr. Leroy Lee Roy? There he is. Leroy! How could you do this to me? Make me follow you around all New York City? In pumps and a thong!

MUHAMMAD. Oh that's just plain disgusting.

DIVINITY. Leroy? Who is this incredibly tall, broad-shouldered man?

SHIRLEY MARKOWITZ. Woman. Shirley Markowitz. I am Leroy Lee Roy's sexual <u>lover</u>.

RABBI NATHAN. This is a new one on me.

MRS. WEINER. We don't even have a section for that.

DIVINITY. Leroy? Is this true? Is this man...

SHIRLEY MARKOWITZ. Woman.

LEROY LEE ROY. What a waste of a perfectly good Brother. I love Shirley Markowitz, Divinity. She has everything I want in a woman. Charm. Education. And a penis.

DIVINITY. Why didn't you tell me?

LEROY LEE ROY. I was too embarrassed. But if the 70s has taught me anything it's that we have to be our own individuals. And stand up for the way God made us. Leroy Lee Roy loves me a *tranny*.

SHIRLEY MARKOWITZ. Pre-op if anyone is really interested.

RABBI NATHAN. We're not really interested.

HAVA. No, we don't care.

DOUGLAS. (*Overlap*) Not our business.

LEROY LEE ROY. So you'll understand if I can't reciprocate your love for me, Divinity?

DIVINITY. You're keepin' it real, Leroy. I respect that.

LEROY LEE ROY. But we can still work together. We make a good couple on the streets. Right?

DIVINITY. (*Looks at WEINER*) You're off the hook, Leroy. Maybe there's other things I can do that would get me psyched up, you know?

SHE marches over to WEINER.

DIVINITY (*CONT'D*). Miss Librarian. I would like to apply for a job here.

MRS. WEINER. Right on, *sista*. I know the lingo too. (*Puts HER hand out*) Slap me some skin.

DIVINITY. No. I just want to fill out an application.

MRS. WEINER. Oh. Okay. (*Softly; SHE hands HER papers*) Just tryin' to join in on the fun jive talk.

LEROY LEE ROY. (*Crosses to WEINER*) Allow me to introduce myself. Leroy Lee Roy. Charmed, sugar. How much money does a girl like you make?

MRS. WEINER. Oh not nearly enough with the budget and all... The library doesn't. Oh. You want me to...you think I could go out on the streets and...Oh, please, Mr. Leroy Lee Roy (*Whispers to HIM*) Let's talk about the details later. (*And SHE winks*)

Lights up on street.

DETECTIVE ISSAC. Tony. I got some news.

TONY runs to the window.

DETECTIVE ISSAC (*CONT'D*). The mayor said you don't get a dime. Next time, rob a place with money.

TONY. Look. "Nobody gets hurt if you listen to what I say." I want a helicopter.

CARLO. We going on vacation, Tony?

DETECTIVE ISSAC. Tony. You gotta do it my way. Let a few of the hostages go and we can talk some more.

TONY. Okay. Okay. Pimp. Go.

LEROY LEE ROY. Oh Leroy Lee Roy does not leave his woman behind.

DIVINITY. Oh, Leroy, that's the sweetest thing—

LEROY LEE ROY. – I was talkin' about the man.

SHIRLEY MARKOWITZ. – Woman.

LEROY LEE ROY. The man/woman.

TONY. Carlo – get them out of here!

CARLO leads LEROY and SHIRLEY out.

TONY (*CONT'D*). (*Out the window*) You got your hostages, detective...now what?

DETECTIVE ISSAC. (*To O'REILLYHULAHANO'BRIEN*) We ready to move in? (*She nods*)

Lights out on street.

GARY. Oh, Zinobia. I've been so unfair to you. Spending my days here when I should have been by your side. And now we're having a baby without a name. I just don't know what I did wrong. I was sure that the clues led me to look for the stash in articles in *L'Humanité*. I even broke down the letters to look under each one individually: L and U and M and A and N and I and T and E. Still nothing.

ZINOBIA. (*Panting heavily*) What about "H"?

GARY. "H"?

ZINOBIA. It's spelled *L-H-u-m-a-n-i-t-é*. In French the "H" is silent.

GARY. The silent French "H". Of course. Somebody, quickly, point me toward the "H's!"

WEINER leads HIM out, leaving ZINOBIA on the floor with HAVA.

ZINOBIA. Is somebody going to get me out of here?

CARLO. Tony. We should let the *preggo* go. You know?

TONY. They're never gonna give us the money if we let everyone go, Carlo.

ZINOBIA lets out a scream.

TONY (*CONT'D*). Fine. *Preggy*, you're next. Carlo – get her up.

ZINOBIA. I can't go. I don't have a baby name yet!

TONY. Okay, okay. How about, ah…I got it. John Merven Carrère Zinger.

ZINOBIA. I like that. Johnny Zinger.

TONY. Now go. Have your baby. Have your happy life. Just do me one favor.

THEY help HER up onto the skates.

TONY (*CONT'D*). Love that kid with all your heart.

A Very Merry Happy Kosher Christmas

HE positions HER and pushes; SHE skates out.

ZINOBIA. I – gotta - pee – again!!

TONY paces. Thinks. HE looks at BERNADETTE and motions.

BERNADETTE. Tony.

TONY. I know. I know.

BERNADETTE. We gave it a good shot. But if I marry you, my life won't have time for studying. Travelling. Experiencing. I'll be a 1980's housewife raising babies. Disco will be over and who knows what cool music the '90s will bring? We all have to grow, Tony. And change. There will be changes. In technology and politics. Some day "late book fees" will cost as much as twenty-five cents a day.

MRS. WEINER. Oh that's a funny one.

BERNADETTE. But for right now.

TONY. Don't say it. (*Beckons*) Carlo.

CARLO walks over.

TONY (*CONT'D*). Take Bernadette and go.

CARLO. Tony.

TONY. You guys belong together. You got a lot in common.

CARLO. (*To BERNADETTE*) We can be together. Me and you and your enormous sniffing ability.

SHE hugs HIM. CARLO and BERNADETTE start to go, but CARLO stops.

CARLO (*CONT'D*). No. I came in with my best friend and I'm going out with him.

BERNADETTE. What if you go to prison, Carlo? We'll never know if we were really meant for each other.

CARLO. Will you wait for me?

BERNADETTE. (*Thinks for a beat*) Not so sure. I'm a pretty hot girl.

MRS. WEINER. I respect your dreams, Bernadette. Burn that bra if you must. You can find your dreams out there. This isn't the 50s anymore. And the radicals of the 60s have come and gone. When I was having indiscriminate sex with many unknown male friends at Woodstock... (*SHE stops HERself*) Oh my. That's a good memory.

BERNADETTE. I love you, Tony. I always will.

SHE hugs TONY again, takes in a huge puff of air; nostrils flaring, and exits, as TONY wipes away a tear.

NATHAN stands in the corner, pulls out a small prayer book and begins to doven. *HE looks next to HIM and notices MUHAMMAD on HIS knees praying towards Mecca. THEY each notice the other.*

SHPILKA. (*Sees PATRICIA trying to sneak out*) Hadassah? What are you doing?

PATRICIA. I am Patricia Vanderbuilt now.

SHPILKA. No. No. You're Hadassah Morgankvelts. You have a man you love. And a son. And your son is over there.

PATRICIA. I can't... I can't face him. I gave him away like a Mobile, Alabama prized calf who grows up not to milk.

SHPILKA. He wants to meet you.

PATRICIA. I have nothing to offer my own son, Shpilka. I am a washed-up ex-Radio City Music Hall dancer. Today I was giving up. Packing my bags back for Mobile, Alabama where I might add the unemployment rate just topped off at a hundred and four percent.

SHPILKA. You know I've always loved you, Hadassah Morgankvelts.

PATRICIA. You loved the <u>idea</u> of loving me, Shpilka Ishmael.

SHPILKA. I love the idea of finally having a life with you.

PATRICIA. It's not just that you want to nail a dancer again?

SHPILKA. It could be that too. Come. Time to face the future, my dear. Time you meet Yachleel Zerubbabbel Ishmael.

SHE nods. SHPILKA walks HER to TONY.

RABBI NATHAN. So...what is it you did over there?

MUHAMMAD. Where?

RABBI NATHAN. With the praying.

MUHAMMAD. Back there.

RABBI NATHAN. What did you pray for?

MUHAMMAD. The Yankees.

NATHAN bursts into laughter. Soon THEY both are laughing.

RABBI NATHAN. Good one. THAT is a good one!

More laughs from BOTH.

RABBI NATHAN (*CONT'D*). You know Rabbi's make mistakes. If I can accept Tony into my family, why can't I let my grown up daughter choose a husband?

TONY. (*Out the window*) These are the last two I let go, flat-foot. (*Turns*) You two lovers. Out.

MUHAMMAD goes to HAVA but SHE takes DOUGLAS' hand as SHE bites HER nails.

MUHAMMAD. Oh no. She's biting her nails.

HAVA. I don't even know your last name, Douglas. Please tell me so I will never forget the name of the most important inventor of the twentieth century.

DOUGLAS. Douglas. Douglas Starbucks.

MUHAMMAD. Hava. Does this mean...?

HAVA. How could we have ever made it work, Muhammad? Can you imagine what <u>your</u> father would say?

MUHAMMAD. You're right, Hava. I didn't want to face the truth and... (*Sings the end of the song*) "Summer dreams... ripped at the seams. But... OH. Those Summer.... Nights..."

RABBI/SHPILKA/PATRICIA. (*Sing with great harmony*) "Tell me more. Tell me more."

SOUND: An orchestra crescendo to "Summer Nights."

HAVA and DOUGLAS exit.

Lights up on street.

DETECTIVE ISSAC. (*Through bullhorn*) Tony. The mayor said you don't get a helicopter. Next time, rob an airport.

TONY. Gosh. I did everything right. I sent out hostages, man. Work with me. Ain't you got any money to help me start a new life? Get out of this city. Fall in love again. Jeez. Gotta be money around here someplace!

SOUND: Books fall, crash to the floor.

GARY enters from the stacks. HE has cash coming from every pocket and seam. <u>A hundred thousand dollars worth</u>.

MRS. WEINER. Mr. Zinger! Your wife went to the hospital...

GARY. May I be excused?

TONY. (*Looks at GARY and the money*) Oh that's wacked. Just go. Get out.

GARY pushes the cash into HIS pockets and CARLO helps HIM to exit.

SHPILKA and PATRICIA move to TONY.

SHPILKA. Tony? I'd like you to meet your mother. Hadassah Morgankvelts.

TONY. (*Playing it cool*) So...you're my mother. *Hachacha Morgani-mechanic.* How's the Toyota dealer and the girls?

PATRICIA. There is no other family, Yachleel.

TONY. I suppose I should be happy to— what the hell is that – a name or a disease?

PATRICIA. It was your name, son. I gave it to you while you suckled my bosoms that one day in the hospital for an excruciatingly long seven hours. I loved you.

While TONY is in an embrace with HIS family, OFFICER O'REILLY-HULAHANO'BRIEN enters and ushers NATHAN, MUHAMMAD and DIVINITY out. WEINER refuses to move from HER desk.

SOUND: Feet running down stairs.

TONY. (*Turns back*) What the hell happened to my hostages?

CARLO. They're all gone, Tony.

TONY. (*Defeated, loudly out the window*) Okay, hostage negotiator... I give up. I'm coming out!

DETECTIVE ISSAC. That's good news. Because I really feel like kicking back with a cold Budweiser and scalping some orchestra seats for tonight's performance of "Hello Dolly." (*To O'REILLYHULAHANO'BRIEN*) Care to join me?

SHE beams ear to ear. But HE's not sure why SHE is so happy.

NATHAN steps out onto the street.

RABBI NATHAN. Issac?

DETECTIVE ISSAC. Poppa?

RABBI NATHAN. Issac. You were right. I don't want to lose Hava. I don't want to lose you. It's time to bond this family. It's what your mother would have wanted.

DETECTIVE ISSAC. Some day, Poppa, you will dance at my wedding. To Bernard.

RABBI NATHAN. I will dance at your gay wedding with Bernard when the Soviet Union breaks into a million little pieces and there's a *shvartza* in the White House!

THEY smile at each other. It begins to snow on them.

RABBI NATHAN (*CONT'D*). Look. It's going to be a white Christmas.

DETECTIVE ISSAC. And I've got my Santa.

HE bear hugs HIS father.

Lights out on street.

SHPILKA. We're gonna be a family, Patricia.

PATRICIA. Call me Hadassah.

TONY. Come on, go go. You're free.

PATRICIA. Tony. You promise me one day when you get out for good behavior, you will come with me and your father to Mobile, Alabama where nothing much happens and racism runs rampant?

TONY. It's a vacation I look forward to.

SHPILKA. Yachleel? Good luck.

TONY. I love you both!

SHPILKA and PATRICIA run out.

CARLO. You think the cops will forgive us for everything, Tony?

TONY. What did we really do wrong? Kept a couple of people in the library for a while the night before Christmas eve.

HE hands CARLO HIS big shoes.

TONY. Thanks, man. I couldn't a done it today without you.

CARLO. We're buddies. It was just a synchronicity of incontrovertible rhetorical discourse. (*THEY stare at each other momentarily*) *Fuhgeddaboutit.*

TONY. (*Overlap*) *Fuhgeddaboutit.*

CARLO starts to go, then stops, puts HIS gun down.

CARLO. Hey, Chief. "Leave the gun. Take the cannoli."

CARLO does the Pinky Tuscadero slap and snap again, then exits.

SOUND: *A barrage of gun fire.*

TONY. Oh good. It's safe.

HE puts the gun down on Weiner's desk, grabs the bag of cannoli, and exits.

SOUND: More gun fire.

WEINER shakes HER head, walks to the window and closes it, then turns back.

SOUND: Some rustling in the corner.

A MAN dressed like a giant snowman enters, right.

HERSCHEL. Shpilka? Nathan? It's me. Herschel! I've decided to join the family business!

MRS. WEINER. *Shhhhh.* This is a library!

Music up: "Pick A Pocket or Two" from the Broadway show – "Oliver."

ON THE SCRIM, we now see written:

Today... Three out of four Americans now own a home computer.

Sales of CD's are down 65%.

-- Although sales of Abba (and the Broadway musical of their music) have sold over 400 million units.

Due to the current economic crisis, The New York Public Library, which contains more than 20 million books, is facing a $23 million dollar funding cut.

Jimmy Hoffa is still missing.

And Liberace was ALWAYS gay.

And... Everyone... I mean everyone... carries a telephone with them.

CURTAIN.

NOTE: During curtain call the entire cast sings the last line of the song.

END OF SHOW.

A Very Merry Happy Kosher Christmas

Other Plays by Mark Troy

The Bitter Herbs
(3m 3f.)
A collection of five short plays that depict American Jewish life for the Passover season that make up one evening of theater. "Mark Troy has an easy way with words... This diverting work concerns heightened situations that any might encounter. The whole evening is a giggle, well-rendered...if it won't make you think, it will make you laugh...and you don't have to be Jewish." Backstage West.

The Secret Nymph of New Hyde Park
(6m 3f.)
A New York Senator finds out his wife has some extra political activities in order to raise money for his run. "'The Secret Nymph' is a wild and woolly romp... go along with a gag, a giggle or a guffaw (in this) zany sex farce and savvy political satire whipped together into a froth of frenzied absurdity." Drama-Logue

Tsuris
(4m 5f.)
Retirement in Century Village never looked so facocked when two lovers meet only to find out their aging parents are having an affair. "Comic tribulations aplenty...over-the-top orgy of Borscht-Belt-flavored slap-stick." IN-Magazine Los Angeles

Paging Dr. Chutzpah
(2m 3f.)
Psychiatrist Lester Oronofsky is New York's most disreputable doctor... and now he has to train his own nephew in his footsteps. "A saucy boulevard romp. A lewd and lunatic study that kicks the Catskills style into a place somewhere between Woody Allen and Hooters. Troy has a talent for outsized patter, and he certainly layers on the situational dynamics." Los Angeles Times

Belladonnas of the Court
(3m 3f.)
When a local L.A. neighborhood is scheduled for demolition, the inhabitants must band together to save what little community pride they have. "Mark M Troy's modernistic reflections on gentrification in LA's Fairfax District commands respect with Ionesco style banter.... It's refreshing." LA Weekly

Desperation
(1m 3f.)
Debbie Zlotnik has no idea what she is getting herself into when she is coupled with Gerald Febermiltz after joining the Insta-Mating Dating Service. It's only a matter of time before she finds out that Gerald has murdered the previous two women the dating service has sent over. "'Desperation' displays a remarkable adroit use of language and characterization in the ingenious exploration of male/female relationships."   Village View

About the Author

Mark Troy is the winner of the Drury International Playwriting Award Prize for *Mr. Wexler* and The Claire Donaldson Prize for Playwriting for the play *Afterpiece*. Produced, New York: *Desperation* (Samuel French Best Short Play), *The Plot* (Riant Festival Winner), *Jewel Avenue* (Writer's Theater), *A Jewish Booty Call* (Theatre-Studio). Los Angeles: *Tsuris, Paging Dr. Chutzpah* (Sidewalk Studio), *Belladonna's of the Court* (Theatre League, Best Comedy Nom., Brooklyn Publishers), *The Secret Nymph of New Hyde Park* (Renegade Theater), *Peking Duck* (Next Stage), *Homewrecker* (Rose Theatre), *Getting You Bupkus, Misguided Production, Shiksa, Join The Club* (Malibu Stage Winners), *Everyone I Know* (L.A. Play Festival Winner). Others: *Century Village Boca, The Proposal, Birdy* (Actors Theatre of Louisville), Balloon (Chicago Dramatist Winner), *Sister Snell* (Acme, Boston), *How To Marry Your Stalker* (Harrogate, England), *Man on the Mountain* (British Columbia). Mark has had over 50 plays produced around the world. *The Plot* is published (Smith & Kraus) Best Plays of 2007, and *Sister Snell*, Best Plays 2008. His collection of short plays under the title *The Bitter Herbs* is published by Tinsel Road Books. Troy is working on his first musical *Who Gets The House* with composer Lenny Solomon and wrote the original screenplay for *Tooth Fairy* and an early draft of *The Guru*. He also co-wrote *Driving Me Crazy* starring Joe Bologna, Mickey Rooney and Celeste Holm and the horror cult classic *Zipperface*. Troy teaches screenwriting and speaks at many writers conferences. He is a member of the WGA and The Dramatist Guild of America. Please visit Mark Troy on the web at www.curtainrise.com.

www.ingramcontent.com/pod-product-compliance
Lightning Source LLC
Chambersburg PA
CBHW031223090426
42740CB00007B/679